DRUGS*

✳ A User's Guide

Thanks to Andrew Goodfellow, Stephen Arnott, Ali Glenny and to all those who have provided suggestions, advice and information – Clive Whichelow, Nick Canner, Nodge Carnegie, Jo Blakeley and all the good people of TSO, Tony Dadoun and Jackie Beavis, Ruth, Eleanor and indeed my mum.

DRUGS*

* A User's Guide

Mike Haskins

EBURY
PRESS

First published 2003 by Ebury Press,
An imprint of Random House,
20 Vauxhall Bridge Road, London SW1V 2SA
www.randomhouse.co.uk

The Random House Group Limited supports The Forest Stewardship
Council (FSC®), the leading international forest certification organisation.
Our books carrying the FSC label are printed on FSC® certified paper.
FSC is the only forest certification scheme endorsed by the leading
environmental organisations, including Greenpeace. Our
paper procurement policy can be found at
www.randomhouse.co.uk/environment

Addresses for companies within The Random House Group Limited can be found
www.randomhouse.co.uk/offices.htm

The Random House Group Limited Reg. No. 954009

Printed and bound in Great Britain by Clays Ltd, St Ives PLC

A CIP catalogue record for this book
is available from the British Library.

Cover designed by Keenan
Interior by seagulls

ISBN 0091887933

MIX
Paper | Supporting
responsible forestry
FSC® C018179

CONTENTS

CONTENTS

CONTENTS

CONTENTS

CONTENTS

CONTENTS

CONTENTS

CONTENTS

HIGH THERE!

Drugs, narcotics, illegal substances, substances of abuse, psychoactive chemicals, uppers, downers, hallucinogens, pot, dope, cannabis, marijuana, hash, ganga, speed, amphetamines, meth, ecstasy, acid, LSD, magic mushrooms, PCP, GHB, steroids, poppers, barbs, heroin, morphine, opium, cocaine, crack, glue, ketamine ...

Yes, people do seem to be doing an awful lot of drugs these days.

For some, drugs are a terrifying menace threatening to rot American and European society from the inside. For others they are a normal part of the daily routine. In 1997 Oasis's Noel Gallagher described taking drugs as like having a cup of tea in the morning. And let's not forget tea itself contains the drug caffeine.

We'll see in this book that drugs, or psychoactive substances, may have been used by mankind – for medical, religious and/or recreational purposes – for tens of thousands of years. There is even evidence to suggest that the Neanderthals used a form of amphetamine.

However, as you may have noticed, in the past hundred years or so the recreational use of drugs has increased astronomically. As the United Nations, no less, has reported, 'at the end of the [nineteenth] century ... due to advances in the field of chemistry and pharmacology, stronger and highly addictive substances such as cocaine and heroin were synthesised. In addition, the invention of hypodermic syringes enabled people to inject these drugs, making their effects more powerful and the risk of addiction more serious.'

Yes, as a race we simply don't know what's good for us. Not only do we stuff ourselves with sweets and junk foods every day, but when it comes to getting off our faces on drugs we're not content with fresh healthy opium poppies and coca leaves. Instead we refine these natural substances into more potent and more dangerous ones, like heroin and cocaine.

In one sense, of course, all drugs, whether legal or illegal, wherever they're from and whatever they're made of, are completely and totally safe and harmless. It's when you put them inside human beings that the trouble starts. Perhaps drugs don't so much change the way people think, feel or

UNTIL recent years, the Inuit (or Eskimos) were the only known people not to use psychoactive substances. The reason was that they were not able to grow anything. This anthropological anomaly ended as soon as alcohol was introduced to them by explorers.

TODAY, large percentages of some countries' gross domestic products are contributed by the drugs trade. An idea of the extremes to which this can run is suggested by the aftermath of a raid on a Colombian cocaine laboratory in 1984. Following the raid, the lab's owners made a tempting offer to the Colombian government. In return for immunity from prosecution they offered to get out their chequebooks and personally pay off the country's entire $13 billion foreign debt.

behave as bring out aspects of the personality that are there anyway. What's more, as we'll find out later in the book, even if you're not full of drugs at this moment, your body will contain substances such as adrenalin, dopamine and endorphins. These naturally occurring chemicals in the body are often stimulated or mimicked by the action of drugs.

This book will also explain how the most popular drugs of abuse used today were first developed, the uses their early champions intended for them, how many of them were openly sold as mass market products and how drugs today have become a legal issue, a health issue and an international industry with a turnover of millions of dollars employing thousands worldwide.

And it's not just human beings. In another chapter we'll expose some of the wild animals which also seem to go out of their way to enjoy the effects of psychoactive plants.

So it looks as if we may have to accept it. Taking drugs is an established activity, alongside eating, drinking, having sex, going to the toilet and dying – not just as a likely précis of the last 24 hours in the life of Elvis but as one of the basic, mundane things that living creatures on this planet get up to.

But just what are these drugs we keep hearing so much about?

According to one book, 'A drug is any substance that by its chemical nature alters the structure or functioning of a living being.' This could, however, refer to anything from heroin to sugar from the kitchen cupboard. And, as the author Andrew Tyler points out, someone who snorts heroin just once each month could even be said to have less of a problem with his or her chosen substance of abuse than someone who eats sugar in cakes, sweets, junk food and drinks every single day.

The main illegal substances of abuse used in the United States and in Europe tend to fall into one of the following groups:

Opiates (that's opium, morphine, heroin and so on) relieve pain, whether physical or mental, with a sense of euphoria thrown in for good measure.

Cerebral depressants (such as barbiturates) relax you and send you to sleep – but may provide a bit of excitement along the way by sending your inhibitions to sleep first (such, for example, is the enduring attraction of alcohol).

Cerebral stimulants (cocaine, amphetamines, etc.) get you going by cranking up your mental and physical energy so you can get more done, enjoy yourself more and all in all feel like one heck of a guy.

Hallucinogens (such as LSD) work in a complex manner on the brain, affecting your perception and interpretation of the world.

HIGH THERE!

In the United States the whole range of illegal drugs are commonly referred to as 'narcotics'. The word narcotic in fact comes from the Greek *narkotikos*, which means 'numbing'. So while drugs such as heroin and opium may be narcotic, drugs such as cocaine and amphetamines are definitely not narcotics but stimulants.

OK, a little more specifically:

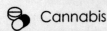

Cannabis

Available as	Hashish (cannabis resin)
	Marijuana (chopped leaves)
	Ganga (chopped leaves, seeds, twigs, etc.)
Obtained from	Varieties of cannabis plants (sativa, indica, ruderalis)
Type of drug	Depressant, hallucinogenic
Means of ingestion	Smoked mixed with tobacco in cigarette papers
	Held between hot knives and smoked
	Swallowed
Active ingredients	Contains over 60 cannabinol compounds, the most psychoactive of which is tetrahydrocannabinol (THC). Hash is usually richer in THC than is marijuana
Takes effect	10 minutes after smoking
	90 minutes after eating

'CANNABIS is by far the most dangerous of all the illicit drugs in its effects upon the authorities. By continuing to penalise it as an innately dangerous substance, despite a lack of supporting evidence they find themselves at odds with literally millions of citizens ...'

– Andrew Tyler

Effects last for	THC clears slowly from the system and may still be in the bloodstream several days after a heavy session
Effects usually felt	Sedative
	Relaxant
	Euphoric
	Mildly hallucinogenic
Or	
	No effects (reported by many first time users)
Possible hazards	Paranoia
	Psychosis and other mental health problems
	Short attention span
	Lethargy and apathy
	Respiratory problems
	Lung cancer

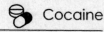

Cocaine

Available as	Cocaine hydrochloride (white crystalline powder)

	Cocaine sulphate (known as pasta, base, paste, etc. – a brown impure mixture produced during the process of refining coca into cocaine powder)
Obtained from	The leaves of varieties of the South American coca plant
Type of drug	Stimulant
Means of ingestion	Chopped finely and inhaled, usually through a rolled banknote, a straw, etc. Can be diluted and injected. Pasta can be smoked
Active ingredients	Cocaine (duh)
Takes effect	In seconds
Effects last for	40 minutes to an hour
Effects usually felt	Stimulation of the central nervous system. Rush of exhilaration. Greatly enhanced self-confidence. Increased mental capacity. Indifference to pain. Increased stamina
Possible hazards	Damage to nasal membranes. Total collapse of part of the nose, for example the septum. Irregular heart rate. Reduction in libido. Psychosis and other mental health problems

Heroin

Available as	Brown powder (adulterated)
	White powder (probably purer)
Obtained from	Derivative of morphine, itself a derivative of opium obtained from the opium poppy
Type of drug	Narcotic
Means of ingestion	Dissolved in liquid and injected under skin, into muscle or into vein
	Snorted
	Smoked off foil
Active ingredients	Diacetylmorphine
Takes effect	In seconds if injected
	In minutes if taken by other means
Effects last for	Three to four hours
Effects usually felt	Initial rush from injection
	Intense warm pleasure spreading from the belly
	Woozy carefree sensation
	Sense of being wrapped in cotton wool or returning to the womb
	Stupefaction and loss of feeling
Possible hazards	Nausea
	Collapsed veins caused by injection
	Disease and other health hazards associated with repeated, inefficiently sterilised injections (for example, collapsed veins, septicaemia,

hepatitis, AIDS, etc.)
Physical addiction
On-going financial, social and health
problems resulting from maintaining
the habit and being regularly stupefied
and desensitised
Overdose

LSD

Available as	Tabs (squares of blotting paper)
	Microdots (small tablets)
	Liquid
Obtained from	Artificially created chemical compound
Type of drug	Hallucinogen
Means of ingestion	Swallowed
Active ingredients	Lysergic acid diethylamide (or in the
	original German *Lyserg saeure*
	diathylamid, hence LSD)
Takes effect	In 30 minutes
Effects last for	Eight to twelve hours
Effects felt	Distortions in perception of the world
	Visual hallucinations
	Intense self-awareness
	Euphoria
	Deep spiritual-like sensations
Possible hazards	Bad trip (inescapable nightmare from
	drug's effects)
	Long-term mental health problems

Crack

Available as	Rocks
	Cocaine hydrochloride (crack is essentially the same drug but in a different, smokable, form and providing faster, more intense effects)
Obtained from	Cocaine hydrochloride mixed with water and heated in a microwave with bicarbonate of soda
Means of ingestion	Smoked from a glass tube or pipe, or off foil
Type of drug	Stimulant
Active ingredients	Cocaine
Takes effect	After a very few seconds
Effects last for	30 minutes
Effects usually felt	Euphoria
	Sense of well-being
Possible hazards	Tiredness
	Psychosis
	Depression
	Respiratory problems
	Lung damage
	Addiction and the on-going financial, social and health problems of maintaining the habit

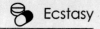 Ecstasy

Available as	Tablets
Obtained from	Artificially created chemical compound
Type of drug	Stimulant, hallucinogen
Means of ingestion	Swallowed
Active ingredients	Methylenedioxymethamphetamine (MDMA)
Takes effect	In 20 minutes
Effects last for	Two to four hours – and sometimes longer
Effects usually felt	Likened to a mixture of LSD and amphetamine effects
	Euphoria followed by feeling of calm (chilling out)
	Enhanced sociability
Possible hazards	Psychosis
	Depression
	Brain damage
	Liver damage

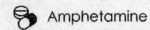 Amphetamine

Available as	Powder
Obtained from	Artificially created chemical compound
Type of drug	Stimulant
Means of ingestion	Snorted
	Injected
	Smoked
	Swallowed
Active ingredients	Amphetamine sulphate
Takes effect	In 15 minutes if eaten
	Faster if taken by other methods
Effects last for	Six hours
	Come-down can last several days
Effects usually felt	Stimulation of the central nervous system
	Exhilaration
	Energy
	Enhanced self-confidence
	Concentration
	Faster mental ability
Possible hazards	Inducement of aggressive behaviour
	Psychosis
	Exhaustion (pay-back time after use)
	Depression
	Heart problems
	Triggering of latent mental conditions such as schizophrenia

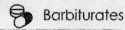 ## Barbiturates

Available as	Pills
Obtained from	Artificially created chemical compound
Type of drug	Sedative, depressant
Means of ingestion	Swallowed
	Injected
	Often combined with amphetamines
	for an up/down effect (famously as
	Purple Hearts in the 1960s)
Active ingredients	Chemical derivatives of barbituric acid
Takes effect	In 15 minutes
Effects last for	Three to six hours
Effects usually felt	Tranquillity
	Loss of inhibition
	Fluctuation of emotion
Possible hazards	Quarrelsomeness and violence
	Chaotic behaviour
	Pneumonia
	Hypothermia
	Emotional disturbance
	Overdose
	Can be lethal if injected

DRUGS may be many things, but one thing they definitely are is extremely popular with a great many people.

A survey in the 1990s by the London listings magazine *Time Out* showed that 97 per cent of its 25-year-old readers used cannabis. Presumably this was because they couldn't find anything better to go out and do in the pages of *Time Out*.

More recently and more scientifically the United Nations estimated that there were around 180 million drug users worldwide. In other words, about one in every 25 adults living on this planet is a druggy.

According to the US National Household Survey in 2000, 24.5 million Americans aged 12 or over (or 11 per cent of the population) had used illicit drugs on one or more occasion during the year. Of these, 2.7 million were black, 2.4 million were Hispanic and the remaining 18.2 million were white.

In spring 2002 the *Observer* newspaper conducted a major survery of drug use in the UK. To the basic question 'have you ever taken an illegal drug?' a staggering 28 per cent of adults questioned replied that they had. If this survey was applied to the entire British population, it would translate into 13 million people who had at some time used drugs. The survey found that around half of this group remained regular drug users.

As regards different types of drugs, the UN found that 9 million people worldwide were heroin addicts, 14 million people were cocaine users (it's the UN that calls cocaine addicts 'users' and heroin users 'addicts' incidentally), 13 million people were opiate abusers (ditto),

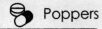 Poppers

Available as	Liquid
Obtained from	Artificially created chemical compound
Type of drug	Stimulant
Means of ingestion	Sniffed
Active ingredients	Amyl, propyl or butyl nitrite
Takes effect	In seconds
Effects last for	A few minutes
Effects usually felt	Rush of energy
	Lowering of inhibitions
	Relaxation of the body (relaxation of the anal sphincter muscle made the drug a particular favourite among gay men)
Possible hazards	Skin disorders from contact with liquid
	Headache
	Nausea
	Blood pressure and heart problems
	Haemorrhage, coma, death

29 million people took amphetamine, and 144 million people were cannabis users.

In Britain and the US, cannabis (marijuana) seemed to be by far the most popular drug. The US Household Survey estimated that 76.3 million Americans had tried cannabis at some point in their lives.

So, essentially, if you want to reduce the worldwide illegal use of drugs by 80 per cent or so overnight, legalise cannabis.

STONED AGE MAN

 The birth of civilisation

Drugs may seem a modern phenomenon, but the fact is they've been around for a long time. Perhaps they weren't always regarded as the problem they now seem. Drug use has been an aspect of human life as far back in history as we can tell. In fact, according to one authority, human civilisation might not have developed at all if it hadn't been for drugs.

The American scientist Carl Sagan came up with a theory that the birth of civilisation could have been kick-started by our ancestors growing a bit of a stash for themselves. Sagan studied pygmies in central Africa, who continued to follow an age-old hunter-gatherer lifestyle. Thus the pygmies never established a regular base for themselves and never purposefully planted or farmed any of the crops they needed. There was, however, one exception. The pygmies thought one plant was important enough to sow and cultivate, and that was hemp, which they used for religious ceremonies.

Sagan suggested that in earlier human history, Stone Age people might have followed a similar pattern. Cannabis could have been the very first crop that was thought important enough to be grown on purpose by humans. Growing hash could have been the beginning of all human agriculture, which, it could be argued, in turn began the development of civilisation.

The idea seems to be borne out by the fact that the pattern observed by Sagan seems to have been repeated around the world. In North America, the Blackfoot traditionally disdained agriculture. But they did grow one plant, tobacco. In Australia, the Aborigines didn't develop agriculture until after the arrival of white people. However, they did show an inordinate amount of interest in one plant, the psychoactive pituri. In the Near East, particularly in Neolithic Jericho, the first cultivated plants could have been narcotic herbs such as mandrake, henbane and belladonna, a.k.a. deadly nightshade. In South America 8,000 years ago, tobacco was first cultivated by Indians in their gardens. The purpose seems to have been to make sure that there was a steady supply of tobacco.

So, again and again, agriculture seems to have been initiated not by the need for food but by the desire for mind-blowing substances. Who says dopeheads never get round to doing anything?

 ## Whizz back in time

Archaeology has also suggested that the earliest drug used by man was not cannabis, opium, coca, or even tobacco or

THE idea that civilisation first developed because humans wanted to get their hands on drugs is controversial enough, but in his book *Food of the Gods* Terence McKenna came up with an even more extreme theory: humans evolved from apes as a direct result of the apes having taken hallucinogenic drugs.

The missing link in the evolution of humanity, claimed McKenna, was the *Stropharia cubensis* mushroom, which contains the hallucinogenic chemical psilocybin. Ancient apes living in the ancient African savannah may have come across this fungi growing on the dung of wild cattle. According to McKenna, 'The mushroom is a totally anomalous object in the grassland environment ... it stands out like a sore thumb.' So African apes living hundreds of thousands of years ago may well have had their minds blown on magic mushrooms. But could the effects still be with us today?

McKenna's theory is that eating stropharia mushrooms helped the apes to develop enhanced eyesight, greater sexual enjoyment, an ability to evolve language and the self-reflective consciousness that distinguishes human beings from animals.

So the mushroom-eaters gained great advantages for their species in the battle for survival. 'Hallucinogenic plants may have been the catalysts for everything about us that distinguishes us from other primates, except perhaps the loss of body hair,' claimed McKenna. 'All of the mental functions that we associate with humanness, including recall, projective imagination, language, naming, magical speech, dance, and a sense of religion may have emerged out of interaction with hallucinogenic plants.'

alcohol. It was speed. And it wasn't used by Homo sapiens; it was used by Neanderthals.

This idea comes from the excavation of a 60,000-year-old Neanderthal grave site at Shanidar in Iraq. Among many other discoveries at the site, one adult male Neanderthal skeleton was found to have been buried surrounded by at least seven species of flowers.

At first it was thought that the flowers had been put there for decoration. In other words, the Neanderthal mourners had been laying flowers at the grave as we do today. After establishing what sort of flowers had been placed in the grave, however, it began to look as though the Neanderthals had not put down plants that looked attractive or smelt fragrant but ones that they used medically.

The main plants discovered in the grave were known to have medicinal properties in Western folk medicine. In fact, the plants are used to this day in the geographical region in which the grave was found. One of the main specimens discovered was woody horsetail or *Ephedra vulgaris*. This is

McKenna was also reliably informed that the stropharia is 'an alien symbiote whose spores were borne across the galaxy'. In fact it was the mushroom itself that passed this nugget on. Admittedly McKenna was tripping at the time. Nevertheless, the distinguished scientist Francis Crick, who was awarded the Nobel Prize for his work on DNA, has also put forward a theory of directed panspermia – all life on earth sprang from spores that arrived here from an extraterrestrial source, possibly engineered by a higher intelligence.

EXCAVATIONS in Thailand and the Philippines, dating from up to 9,000 years ago, have produced skeletons with their teeth stained black. This was not the result of poor dental care but of chewing betel nuts, a stimulant still used by around 10 per cent of the world's population. Traditionally, in the Philippines black teeth from heavy betel chewing were a sign of social status.

a herb with stimulant properties similar to those of amphetamines or ecstasy. In prehistoric temples in central Asia, ephedra remains have been found, suggesting that they were used with more potent substances such as cannabis and opium. In fact, ephedra's active ingredient, ephedrine, is today the basis of 'herbal ecstasy' pills, available for sale on the Internet and in specialist magazines.

So the Iraqi Neanderthal grave could be the earliest instance found of the medicinal use of herbs by human beings. The idea that Neanderthals were using herbal ecstasy really does suggest that the 'Just Say No' campaign is battling against the tide of history, doesn't it?

Ancient opium

Opium seems to have been been cultivated from about 6000 BCE. These days, the farming of opium poppies is mainly associated with Near Eastern countries such as Turkey and Afghanistan. Recent research, though, suggests that opium poppies could actually be native to southern France and

Spain and were first cultivated in the eastern reaches of Europe, such as the Balkans or around the Black Sea.

Opium poppy seeds have been discovered inside a 7,000-year-old religious artefact found in Spain, while lakeside dwellers in Switzerland around 2500 BCE were the first Europeans known to eat the flower's produce. By the Iron Age, opium poppies seem to have been grown even in countries such as Britain and Poland.

As long ago as 5000 BCE, one group of people definitely knew about the effects of opium. In Sumeria, part of modern-day Iraq, ancient ideogram symbols have been discovered that seem to depict the opium poppy. The Sumerian word represented by this symbol is *hul gil* or 'plant of joy'.

The earliest actual find of opium comes from Egypt and the three-and-a-half-thousand-year-old tomb of an architect called Cha, who lived during the reign of Pharaoh Amenhotep III. Inside Cha's tomb was found an alabaster bucket containing a preparation. On analysis, one of the substances in the bucket turned out to be opium.

 ## Egyptian drugs

As well as opium, the Egyptians were also known to be keen users of mandrake and cannabis. At the grand temple of Karnak, the walls are covered with depictions of the blue lotus flower. For years it was presumed that ancient Egyptian use of blue lotus was confined to religious ceremonies and that it was some kind of powerful narcotic. Ancient Egyptian art often shows individuals dropping lotus flowers into cups of wine to release the plant's intoxicating ingredients. Recent analysis, however, has shown that the lotus, unlike the opium poppy, does not contain any chemicals with narcotic effects. It stimulates the body in a different way. The blue lotus was not the Egyptians' heroin or cocaine, it was their Viagra.

Art in Egyptian tombs was not created for mere decoration. Pictures were painted on the walls of the tombs to help in the eventual rebirth of the dead buried there. Male Egyptian mummies were often buried with artificial phalluses attached to them, while the lotus, with its ability to stimulate the blood flow, aided the reborn dead to get back in the business of procreation. Also, as a panacea against disease akin to ginseng, the lotus would have provided much-needed help in combating the immense range of diseases and afflictions suffered by individuals at every level of society in the ancient world.

Two substances that it should definitely have been impossible for the ancient Egyptians to have access to were nicotine and cocaine. These, of course, could only have been obtained from plants growing in South America, thousands of miles away across the unchartered Atlantic Ocean. Nicotine, famously, did not cross the Atlantic until the time of Francis Drake, while cocaine was not used in the West until Victorian times. Yet one case suggests that the ancient Egyptians knew all about them.

The mystery of the 'cocaine mummies' begins in Thebes 3,000 years ago when the body of a woman called Henut Taui, the Lady of the Two Lands, was mummified and buried. After her tomb was plundered in the 19th century, her remains ended up in a museum in Munich.

There, in the early 1990s, repeated scientific tests showed that Henut Taui's ancient Egyptian body definitely contained hefty quantities of both cocaine and nicotine.

Further examination of the body showed that this was a genuine ancient Egyptian mummy, not a fake, and that the drugs were also in the shafts of the woman's hair. In other words, she had definitely consumed the drugs during her lifetime.

The mystery deepened with the examination of 134 bodies from another part of the ancient Egyptian empire, the Sudan. Although these bodies all long pre-dated Columbus's voyage to America, a third of them were found to contain both nicotine and cocaine.

Perhaps there was an ancient trade link between Egypt and America. Historians, though, find this idea unfeasible. Could there have been a strain of tobacco that grew in Africa but which has now been lost? Could there have been other drugs available that were known in the ancient world but which are now also lost for ever? The mystery remains.

THE Egyptians are the first people on record as having a brewery and wine-making establishment – 5,500 years ago. Alcohol use, though, must almost certainly date back to prehistoric times, with the accidental discovery of the effects of fermented plants. About five and a half thousand years ago, people in the eastern Mediterranean are known to have drunk wine from metal vessels, and from there alcohol use spread across Neolithic Europe. At first, alcohol was apparently used in conjunction with opium poppies and cannabis. Gradually, however, it seems to have displaced the other psychoactive substances that were in use.

The Chinese

The ancient Chinese are known to have been experts at growing cannabis. Records survive of how they sowed hemp seeds closely together to produce the tallest strongest crops. *Pen-ts'ao Ching*, the Chinese Emperor Shen Nung's medical compendium compiled in 2727 BC, contains the first written record of cannabis use. The work shows how the hemp plant really did contain something for the entire ancient Chinese family. It provided not only the fibre for fishing nets, mats and clothes, but also oils for cooking, as well as tonics for malaria, beri beri, constipation, rheumatic pains, absent-mindedness and what were described as female disorders – or, in other words, period pains.

As well as popularising 1,001 uses for cannabis, Shen Nung also, according to legend, first brewed up that other, rather more socially acceptable drugs hit, the nice cup of tea. Ancient Chinese tradition tells of how Shen Nung possessed a transparent belly, which surely must have been something of a talking point at dinner parties. One day, after eating green leaves from a tree, the Emperor noticed they had started swimming around inside him. After a while of this, he

CANNABIS is actually native to central Asia, but by the earliest recorded times it had spread not only east to China but also west. A 5,000-year-old burial site in Romania was found to contain a small ritual brazier which still contained the remains of charred hemp seeds.

found his see-through stomach had been thoroughly cleansed. The refreshing and restorative powers of the leaves were thereby established. Shen Nung was the first to name them *cha*. In Britain, of course, people still enjoy a nice cup of 'char' to this day.

South American anaesthetic

In South America, evidence has been found of the use of coca 5,000 years ago. Scientists believe that coca leaves had been chewed for a couple of thousand years before this, since around the time llamas became domesticated. Those llamas have got a lot to answer for.

It wasn't until the 19th century that the use of cocaine as a local anaesthetic was discovered in Western Europe. In ancient Peru, though, the Incas and pre-Inca people seem to have been ahead of the game. Evidence suggests that masticated coca was used as a local anaesthetic prior to what was the most widely performed major surgical operation of the time: trepination.

Trepination, or trepanning, is the process of drilling a hole through the skull. More precisely, it involves the removal of one or more parts of the skull without damaging the blood vessels, the membranes that envelop the brain or, for that matter, the brain itself. The Incas' trepanning tool was a scraper called a tumi, sometimes made of obsidian, sometimes of metal. Yes, you may well say you'd need this like you'd need a hole in the head, but the ancient inhabitants of South America had this operation performed on them regularly. Even more surprisingly, trepanned individuals survived their operations more often than not.

One study of 214 trepanned skulls showed that well over 50 per cent had healed completely afterwards, 16.4 per cent had died in the initial stages of healing and 28 per cent had showed no signs of healing. Another study of 400 trepanned individuals' remains showed that the skulls of 250 of them had healed up at least to some extent following the operation. One skull has been found with no less than five trepanned holes in it. Only one of the holes showed any signs of infection, so the first four trepanations, presumably, had been successful.

So the anaesthetic and indeed the antiseptic the Incas used for the operation must have worked. Because the use of coca was so fundamental to Inca culture and because it possesses both anaesthetic and antiseptic properties, it seems highly likely that this is what they were using. No wonder trepanning operations were so popular.

 ## High culture

A little while later, back in the Mediterranean, the ancient Greeks used many of the psychoactive substances known today, but not always for the reasons that might be expected. Juice extracted from cannabis seeds, for example, was widely used by the citizens of ancient Athens to ease the digestion and prevent after dinner flatulence.

The use of performance-enhancing drugs is not just a feature of recent sporting events. The ancient Olympics

STONED AGE MAN

CONSUMING the testicles of a beast was perhaps thought to pass on the power and strength of the animal. It would, indeed, make an athlete 'the dog's bollocks'. Perhaps, more prosaically, it provided a boost of testosterone such as might be obtained from steroids today. The development of anabolic steroids in the 20th century dates back to 1927, when Fred Koch, a chemist at Chicago University, developed a form of testosterone by extracting the hormone from bull testicles and treating it with benzene and acetone.

involved an extraordinary range of doping regimes. Athletes' preparation obviously involved months of hard training, but the ancient Olympians also knew all about energy-giving diets, stimulant herbs and even muscle-building drugs. Competitors in training for the Games would eat special diets of, for example, dried figs, and take mushrooms and seed potions to help enhance their performance. Then, to really give himself the edge over his opponents, an athlete might consume one or two sheep or dog testicles.

Opium was thought by the ancient Greeks to be so good, they named it twice, if not thrice. In Homer's epic poem *The Odyssey*, Odysseus's son, Telemachus, visits Menelaus in Sparta. During a banquet, when the assembly start to get a bit misty-eyed over Odysseus and all their other loved ones who had been lost in the Trojan war, Helen, daughter of Zeus, pours a drug, nepenthe, into the wine they are drinking.

The nepenthe, according to Homer, 'made them forget all evil. Those who drank of the mixture did not shed a tear all day long, even if their mother or father had died, even if a brother or beloved son was killed before their own eyes by the weapons of the enemy. And the daughter of Zeus possessed this wondrous substance, which she had been given by Polydamma, the wife of Thos of Egypt, the fertile land which produced so many balms, some beneficial and some deadly.' Yes, it was opium. And, as any heroin addict will surely tell you, it helps you forget all your problems.

Several centuries later, the Greek philosopher Theophrastus came up with a different name for the substance. Poppy juice, obtained by crushing the whole plant and usually taken in wine or in honey and water, was called *meconion*. The name he conjured up for the sap extracted from the poppy pod caught on even better, albeit with a little adaptation. Theophrastus was the man who named poppy juice *opion*.

One major event when psychoactive substances were used in the ancient Greek world was the rites of Eleusis. These have been described by some historians as the peak experience of the Greeks and the means by which they regularly opened 'a space in the human psyche for God to enter'.

The 10-day ceremony held at Eleusis, a site just west of Athens, was a symbolic re-enactment of the grain goddess Demeter's journey to the underworld to claim her daughter Persephone back from death. After half a year of preliminary rites and a pilgrimage to Eleusis, the celebrations would climax with a dramatic re-enactment of Demeter and Persephone's story. This performance was enhanced with a mysterious drink called *kykeon*. According to writers, including Homer and Cicero, kykeon did indeeed deliver quite a kick, and the hallucinatory visions and ecstasy it provided did not fade from the memory.

Theories abound as to the ingredients of kykeon. Some suggest a clue to the recipe's basic ingredient might be found in a detail of the story of Demeter and Persephone. The myth tells of how Demeter, like Homer's heroes in *The Odyssey*, forgot her sorrows once she had tasted the gum from the poppy pod.

Others claim that kykeon was a more innocent-sounding concoction of barley and mint. This may sound like something served up in a health food café, but the Greeks had mind-blowing barley. The barley they used had the mould ergot growing on it, and in the 20th century ergot was the substance from which the hallucinogenic compound LSD was derived. Demeter may often have been depicted with poppies, but don't forget she was also the goddess of grain.

Initiates at Eleusis were forbidden on pain of death to tell what they'd seen during the sacred rites. Some, of course, blabbed, and even began celebrating the sacred mysteries at home. One initiate may have got into considerable trouble for using the sacred brew kykeon recreationally. Some commentators argue that it was the great philosopher Socrates who gave away the secret recipe. As a result, the authorities in Athens turned against him, and he was tried and sentenced to death.

Death, on the other hand, was the excuse for drug use for the Scythian people, who lived north of the Black Sea. Following the death of a king, the Scythians would erect a series of small teepee-like tents to celebrate the funeral.

Then, out came the potent substances. The Greek historian Herodotus, writing in 450 BCE, described how on such occasions, the Scythians took hemp seeds and would then 'creep under the cloths and put the seeds on the red-hot stones; but this being put on smokes, and produces such a steam, that no Grecian vapour-bath would surpass it. The Scythians, transported by the vapour, shout aloud.'

The Thracians, from north-east Greece, used cannabis in a similar manner. Thracian sorcerors burned cannabis flowers, as well as other pyschoactive plants, to produce a mystical incense used to induce trances. The sorcerors' abilities were attributed to the 'magical heat' produced from burning the plants, as the Thracians believed the plants dissolved in the flames and then reassembled themselves inside the person who had breathed in the fumes.

Roman excess

In Roman times, Virgil mentions opium in his poems, *The Aeneid* and *The Georgics*, as being used as a sleeping draught. Opium was also associated with Ceres, the Roman goddess of fertility, and is known to have been used as pain relief during childbirth.

In the medical world of the ancient Romans, opium was used, along with other drugs, to minimise patients' screaming and attempts to fight the doctor off during surgery. Opium was used to numb the patient and limit movement, while henbane induced sleeping, if not amnesia, and mandrake slowed the heart rate and deadened pain. The other important

Top 10 drugs used in ancient Rome to induce euphoric trances:

Opium (pain relief, poison, means of self dispatch and drug of abuse even in Ancient Rome)

Mandragora (also known as mandrake – said to provoke delirium and madness and used in ancient times as a soporific and an anaesthetic)

Belladonna (or deadly nightshade – used as a sedative but also capable of paralysing the central nervous system and causing excitement and delirium along the way)

Henbane (from the same Solanaceae plant family as mandrake – used as a sedative but can provoke intoxication followed by narcosis and hallucinations)

Thorn apple (another member of the Solanaceae family – can cause giddiness and delirium)

Hemlock (a member of the same plant family as parnsips and carrots but possessing sedative, antispasmodic and narcotic properties – frequently used in the ancient world as a poison)

Aconite (another highly poisonous plant – used as a painkiller and can cause giddiness and slow the heart rate)

Cannabis (the perennial medicinal recreational favourite largely imported into Ancient Rome from Babylonia)

Alcohol (ever popular depressant and inhibition suppressant)

Mushrooms (as today, sometimes mind blowing, sometimes lethal) aid used by Roman surgeons was speed – getting the operation done as quickly as possible.

Also, in Roman times opium was popular as a poison, and was used as a relatively pleasant means of self-despatch. Opium was the means used by the Emperor Hannibal to meet his end. Pliny considered it quite proper for the infirm elderly to end their miserable lives by a quick overdose of opium. Alternatively, the drug was used to get rid of enemies, friends, family or just about anyone else. The Emperor Claudius's last wife, Agrippina, disguised a lethal dose of the drug in wine and so used it to murder Claudius's son and heir, Britannicus. Agrippina's own child, Lucius Domitius, thus came to rule Rome and is remembered by history as the Emperor Nero. You see how bad drugs are for you.

On the streets of ancient Rome, opium is known to have been openly on sale from shopkeepers and itinerant quack doctors. It was also during the Roman period that the method of opium extraction was perfected that is still used in opium-producing countries today. Nevertheless, the Greeks and the Romans do not seem to have spread the production and use of the drug throughout their empires. The broader international championing of this class A drug came some centuries later.

After the demise of the Greek and Roman empires, the opium trade was established by Arab traders. The Arab physician Avicenna is known to have recommended the drug as a treatement for diarrhoea and diseases of the eye. Presumably, he must have suffered badly from both of these, as he is believed to have been an opium addict and to have died from an overdose. Such health scares did not, however, affect the trade in opium, which the Arabs established throughout Persia, India, China, parts of North Africa and Spain. The opium trade even spread into the heart of Europe following the Arab conquest of the 10th and 11th centuries and the subsequent crusades.

And as we now know, this first hundred thousand years or so of human drug abuse was only just the beginning ...

IT'S ONLY NATURAL

 Naturally occurring substances

The late, great Bill Hicks pointed out that if you think smoking dope is wrong, it's like saying God made a mistake. Cannabis is a naturally occurring plant. 'Oh my me!' Hicks imagined God saying. 'What have I done? I've left pot all over the place! That's going to give people the idea they're supposed to use it or something. Shit! Now I'm going to have to create Republicans!'

And cannabis is only one of thousands of naturally occurring psychoactive substances. If you were of a botanical frame of mind, you could construct a specially designed garden for yourself. On the other hand, while your back garden might end up with a street value of thousands of pounds, it might not be the prettiest of plots.

A weed in the garden

Cannabis is not called the evil weed for nothing. American drug enforcement agents were horrified, in the first part of the 20th century, to find it growing wild at the side of rural roads. In the world of illegal drugs, cannabis may find itself associated with heroin, cocaine and the rest. In plant terms, however, it is a member of the more innocent-sounding mulberry family.

Cannabis is a green bushy plant with saw-toothed leaves and fluted stalks. If you're not already aware of what the plant looks like from images on badges and T-shirts, you can check the cover of your copy of *Sergeant Pepper*. Supposedly, the neat row of plants in front of the Beatles and their friends on Peter Blake's cover includes a selection of cannabis specimens.

Some say that all cannabis plants are members of one genus, *Cannabis sativa*. Sativa means 'most useful' in Latin, and cannabis has, indeed, proved a fantastically useful plant over thousands of years. As well as having medical properties, cannabis – or hemp, as it is also known – has been used for making rope, cloth, sails and paper. In 1776 the American Declaration of Independence was written on hemp paper. It can also be used in the production of varnishes, soaps, fuels and so on.

The different types of cannabis plants vary in size. The sativa can grow to a lanky 6 metres (20 feet), while the indica usually only grows to around just over 1 metre (3 or 4 feet). Of the other varieties, the ruderalis is a tough and stocky plant,

CANNABIS – Are You Sure It's Still Illegal?

Of all the illegal drugs cannabis is the most popular by far – a sub-culture that may well have outgrown its 'sub' prefix.

In Europe and the USA organisations have been set up to promote sometimes frivolous, sometimes very serious causes related to the use of cannabis. The Legalise Cannabis Alliance works to make the legalisation of cannabis a major issue in British politics, Hempire Cafés' aim is to open places where people can smoke (but not purchase) cannabis while THC4MS exists to supply medicinal cannabis chocolate to help alleviate the suffering of multiple sclerosis. In the United States groups such as NORML (The National Organisation for Reform of Marijuana Laws), the American Cannabis Society and the Chicago American Cannabis Society work to change attitudes to this drug. At the same time organisations such as the North American Industrial Hemp Council and the United Hemp Council suggest all the gravitas of American big business. The US even boasts an annual marijuana harvest festival in Weedstock held annually in Madison, Wisconsin.

Among the thousands of books published on the subject of cannabis, the drug has its bible in Jack Herer's *The Emperor Wears No Clothes: The Authoritative Historical Record of Cannabis and the Conspiracy Against Marijuana* if not in Jason King's more literally titled *The Cannabible*. *High Times* magazine regularly features almost porn-like centrefolds of particularly prodigious cannabis bushes. Growing guides also abound with Jorge Cervantes the apparent guru of hemp horticulture with published works such as *Marijuana Indoors: Five Easy Gardens* and *Marijuana Outdoors: Guerilla Growing*. Other pot boilers on which can be found growing wild by the roadside in central Asia. Its seeds are even capable of surviving harsh Russian winters. The sativa on the other hand likes a lot of light, and that's why it grows so well in such sunny climes as Thailand, Colombia, Nigeria, Morocco and Jamaica.

the subject include cookery books (e.g. *Gourmet Cannabis Cookery: The High Art of Marijuana Cuisine*), guides to health and well-being (*The Healing Magic of Cannabis*), tales of woe (*I Was a Government Licensed Medical-Marijuana Salesman Busted by the Federal Government*), practical guides (*The Joint-Rolling Handbook*), guides for the elite (*The Connoisseur's Handbook of Marijuana*) and even guides for older users (*Grandpa's Marijuana Handbook: A User Guide for Ages 50 & Up*).

Various businesses abound particularly on the web to supply accoutrements to marijuana enthusiasts. These include the splendidly titled W H Spliff, Ganjaland, Yahooka.net which models itself on internet giant Yahoo and Britain's 3 Counties Hydroponics whose name suggests a down-to-earth domestic service company.

Recent busts on cannabis growers in Britain and the United States include the regular discovery of plants grown in peoples' homes, the uncovering of hundreds of plants growing in a warehouse development in Stoke-on-Trent and the seizure of one of the world's biggest and most literal marijuana farms in Baltimore where the growing of 3,000 cannabis plants had been disguised to look a cornfield.

All in all you have to admit this is one weed that has found some extraordinarily wily ways to ensure its seeds flourish.

IN summer 2000 Parliament Square, the traffic-surrounded patch of grass outside the Houses of Parliament in central London, was cordoned off by police when several cannabis plants were found forcing their way up through the turf. The seeds had been planted a few months earlier by guerilla gardeners during May Day protests. Around the same time, police also raided no less a residence than Buckingham Palace, where cannabis was found growing in the kitchens. Presumably, the seed had wafted in on the breeze from Parliament Square.

Cannabis is an adaptable plant that thrives best in rich, fertile, neutral to slightly alkaline, well-drained silt or clay loams with moisture-retentive subsoils. And it does seem pretty hardy.

 ## Ephedra

Cannabis, like many of us, is perhaps more useful than good-looking. On the other hand, if you plant some ephedra in your drugs garden, it might make your cannabis look positively beautiful by comparison.

Ephedra is the source of the naturally occurring stimulants ephedrine, pseudoephedrine and norspeudoephedrine, which resemble amphetamines in their effect. It is an odd-looking, botanically primitive shrub. In fact, it's so primitive that it's a practically leafless plant, with tough, jointed, barkless, yellowy-green stems and branches. You can find it growing on the tundra and on the rocky and sandy slopes of

Europe, Asia and America. Ephedra grows to about 30 centimetres (1 foot) high and produces tiny yellow-green flowers and then poisonous, seed-filled, fleshy red cones resembling berries.

As *ma huang* ephedra has been used in traditional Chinese medicine since around 3000 BCE, when physicians started prescribing ephedra tea. As a medicine, ephedra has principally been used for conditions such as bronchial asthma, nasal congestion and sinusitis. It opens the bronchial passages, stimulates the heart and increases blood pressure, metabolic rate, perspiration and urine production. Ephedra has also been used as an energy-booster, a weight-loss supplement and an athletic performance enhancer.

When the Mormons arrived in Utah in 1847, the indigenous people introduced them to the Native American variety of ephedra, in the form of a piney-tasting tonic beverage. The Mormons used it as a substitute for coffee and tea, and it therefore came to be referred to as Mormon Tea. If you're not allowed caffeine, why not take speed instead?

 ## A shrub

OK, now let's really boost the financial value of our shrubbery.

Erythroxylum coca is another extraordinarily ordinary-looking shrub. Dominic Streatfield in his book *Cocaine: An Unauthorised Biography* could not overestimate just how ordinary it looks. BBC correspondent John Simpson described it as having leaves 'like a Putney privet hedge'.

Others have described the coca plant as looking a bit like a camellia. It produces creamy-white flowers, a bit like apple blossom, and its leaves are elliptical and have underneath them two distinctive white lines. Strangely appropriate when you think about it.

The coca plant can supposedly grow to about 3 metres (9 feet) tall. Streatfield, though, says that in reality you'll probably only see them about 1 metre (3 feet) tall, and while the plant is supposed to produce small bright red seeds once a year, you're unlikely ever to see it fruit.

The *Erythroxylum* genus contains something like 250 species of different coca plants. Perhaps a little less than half of these contain active amounts of cocaine and only a small percentage contain enough cocaine to make commercial cultivation worthwhile.

Of the different species, the coca that grows in Bolivia and which at one time dominated the world market is simply called coca. Other species include ipadu, which traditionally grew in the Amazon basin, and novogranatense. Novogranatense gets it name from the South American country where it was found: Nueva Granada, or New Granada, or – these days – Colombia.

Yet another variety of the coca plant is truxillense or, as it was known to the Incas, Royal coca. This small, dark-leaved plant grows only in remote and dry reaches of desert coasts – for example, on the western slopes of the Andes. In fact, it grows in such arid conditions that it's pretty much entirely reliant on human beings for survival. Even if you're not an aficionado of coca or cocaine, truxillense is the plant you're probably most familiar with. This is the plant that is used to flavour Coca-Cola. But before you rush out to buy a case-load, remember that these days they remove the cocaine element before they put coca in the drink.

In his book *A Mad World, My Masters*, John Simpson describes visiting a coca market deep in the Amazon. Surprisingly, when Simpson visited the remote village of Remolino, he found all the local shops selling lawn strimmers, just as you might find at your local DIY store. This was not, however, because the locals all had tidy front gardens to keep in order but because the strimmers were needed to cut the masses of coca leaves into shreds, ready to be made into paste and sold to dealers.

The process of turning the coca into paste is carried out by a coca cook, or *cocinero*, and is in itself a highly danger-ous, potentially explosive job. After stripping the leaves, they are dunked in a plastic pit with a solution of water and sulphuric acid. These are then trodden, with bare feet, three or four times a day until the leaves turn grey and the fluid is drawn off. The liquid is then mixed with lime water, petrol, sulphuric acid, potassium permanganate and ammonia until it is filtered, and the results are dried on a large sheet. The product is cocaine base, the low-grade brown cocaine 'pasta' consumed in South American slums.

Dealers take the paste to laboratories in Colombia, Mexico, the USA or Europe for processing into cocaine powder. By this time the product has, of course, greatly inflated in price. The growers and processors earn something like 0.05 per cent of the total profits – of an industry that wouldn't exist without them.

As for the plant itself, in a hot dry region where nutritional vegetation is scarce, the prevalence of coca is a godsend. Analysis of the leaves shows that they are packed with calcium, iron, phosphorus and vitamins A, B and E, while the greenery is rich in thiamine, riboflavin and vitamin C. So coca is like a freely available, naturally occurring vitamin shot for the locals. The normal intake for Indians in the area is around two ounces of leaves a day. This provides them with virtually all the vitamins they need to survive.

And of course coca leaves provide a bit more than just that. They're also a stimulant and an aid to respiration. This is handy if you're toiling high up in the thin air of the mountains. Coca is also renowned as a bit of an aphrodisiac. So all in all it seems to contain everything you could possibly need for a full and active day in the Andes. Ninety-nine per cent of the coca leaf is *not* cocaine but vitamin- and mineral-packed green stuff. Perhaps it is typical of mankind to discard the healthy bits.

 ## Flowers shooting up

Back in our drugs garden, what flowers could be prettier than some opium poppies or, to give them their technical name, *Papaver somniferum*. That's *somniferum*, the bringer of sleep. But is the opium poppy genuinely naturally occurring? Some say it only exists because of centuries of cultivation by humans. Others say it occurred, or at least mutated, naturally – from the wild poppy that grows just about everywhere in Europe. All 'ordinary' poppies contain very small quantities of opium. Apart from the paper Remembrance Day ones, that is.

The opium poppy takes about 120 days to grow. It likes a rich, well-cultivated, sandy loam soil, a bit of shelter, not too much shade and a temperate climate. Twelve hours of sunlight or more a day is ideal, with not too much rainfall early in its growth. Beyond that it's not fussy. It doesn't need much, if anything, in the way of irrigation, fertiliser, fungicide or pesticide.

The plant grows to between 90 and 150 centimetres (3 and 5 feet) tall and produces a white, red or purple flower. The plant's pod contains two things – seeds and opium – the former for procreation and the latter to serve as a deterrent against pests or perhaps, if you are of a suspicious frame of mind, to wipe out mankind once and for all and reclaim the Earth for plants.

The harvesting of opium is still done according to a technique perfected in Roman times. Two weeks after the petals drop, the pods on the plants are examined. These should now have darkened from their original grey-green colour and have grown to about 5–7.5 centimetres (2–3 inches) wide. If the points of a pod's crown are standing straight out or curving up it is ready, and tapping commences. Tapping is performed with a knife comprising three parallel blades on a handle, which is run over the sides of the pod neither too deeply and not too shallowly. Milky white raw opium then starts to ooze from the pod, turning eventually to a sticky brown gum. The gum is later scraped from the plant with a knife and dried in the sun to a sticky brown substance which is moulded and stored as cakes or blocks of opium.

Now that's a way to get the youngsters into church ...

The top drug-using religions of the world are:

Rastafarianism – a Jamaican faith that emerged in the 1930s and which regards cannabis, or ganja, as the 'holy herb' and uses it as a sacrament in a way likened to the use of communion wine in Christian services. It is based on ideas of equality of all people and a rejection of Western consumerism in favour of more natural lifestyles.

Santo Daime Church – founded in Brazil in 1930, with a doctrine based on Christianity, local nature religions and native Indian beliefs. Members of the church use the natural psychoactive ayahuasca, or yage, made from vine bark and plant leaves, to produce visions and spiritual experiences. This is psychedelic, ecological Christianity working to save the rainforest.

Barquinha – a smaller offshoot of Santo Daime, with its main base in a floating church on the Amazon. Again combines the use of ayahuasca with Christianity and Amazonian religion, but with the addition of African Umbanda spirituality.

Uniao de Vegetal – a third Brazilian Christian nature church involving the use of ayahuasca. This one was founded in 1961, although its members claim the faith dates back to around 1000 BC. Its rituals involve longer periods of silence than those of Santo Daime, as members seek self-knowledge through concentration and the effects of ayahuasca.

Gnostisismo Revolutionario de la Concienca de Krishna – a shamanic community established in the 1980s in the Colombian jungle. This is an ecologically and politically minded group related to the

Gnostic movement. The use of ayahuasca twice a week provides members with a spirit guide.

Bwiti – a religion that has developed in Gabon since the mid-19th century and which combines Christianity with the use of the iboga root, also used in traditional pygmy religion. Consumption of iboga stimulates the body while higher quantities can cause individuals to enter trance states.

The Native American Church, or Peyotism – has over 250,000 members. It combines Christian and native beliefs teaching brotherly love, high moral principles, and abstention from alcohol. There is a patron saint of peyote called El Santo Niño Peyotl. The peyote itself is viewed by the church as a sacrament through which God manifests Himself to man.

Temple of the True Inner Light – a New York offshoot of the Native American church, based on Catholic dogma reinterpreted through the use of the synthetic psychedelic DPT (dipropyltyramine). The temple sees DPT not only as its sacrament but also as the actual manifestation of God.

And it might be argued that by virtue of the use of wine, incense, etc., many branches of the established Christian church also have an interest in psychoactive effects. Nevertheless, the theory put forward in John Allegro's book *The Sacred Mushroom and the Cross* is probably pushing things a little too far. Allegro argues that the biblical stories of Jesus are all in fact coded references to an ancient cult based on the use of *Amanita muscaria* hallucinogenic mushrooms. As Nicholas Saunders politely puts it in his work *In Search of the Ultimate High*, 'This theory is very controversial and has not received much support from other scholars of religion.'

Peyote

To make your garden a little more exotic, how about a peyote cactus? The peyote is a native of Mexico and contains more than 50 psychoactive ingredients, the most powerful and renowned of which is mescaline. Although as a hallucinogen mescaline is 4,000 times less powerful than LSD, it works in a similar manner on the brain. A dose provides a trip of about 10 hours involving a rush of physical energy followed by lethargy as well as kaleidoscopic visionary hallucinations and possible profound spiritual experience.

Peyote was brought into the USA by raiding parties of Mescalero Apaches who used it for religious and healing rituals. A cult developed out of these rites and ultimately a formal church was established. The peyote church had to do legal battle with the American authorities before the federal government upheld the members' right to carry on using hallucinogenic cacti.

Mescaline has proved a particular hit with writers. It's the drug Aldous Huxley celebrated in his 1954 book *The Doors of Perception* for its mystical and spiritually cleansing qualities. William Burroughs in *Junky* describes how to turn the mescaline-producing buttons on the head of the cactus into something almost, but not quite, edible. Burroughs relates how bark and fuzz were peeled off the peyote buttons before they were run through a grater until they looked 'like avocado salad'. According to Burroughs, about four buttons was enough for a beginner. Even after this much, however, the *Junky* himself began to feel very sick indeed. While Bill's companions instructed him to, 'Keep it down, man', eventually he had to head for the WC. There he found his cactus gratings wouldn't come up and nor would they stay down. Eventually they re-emerged 'solid like a ball of hair'. An event Burroughs described as being 'as horrible a sensation as I ever stood still for'.

Peyote can be consumed in the mouth-watering recipe Burroughs outlined or made into tea. Its effects can be colourful visions and hallucinations or, as Burroughs described it, something like a Benzedrine high after which he couldn't sleep, his pupils dilated and everything he saw began to look like a peyote plant.

 ## Betels to morning glory

The Asian betel nut palm, *Areca catechu*, will provide you with a crop of betel nuts. These can be chewed with peppermint or some other leaf and some slaked lime and will provide a mild euphoria as well as permanently blackened teeth. West African yohimbine tree bark can also be eaten, smoked, sniffed or brewed up in tea for euphoria, hallucinations, increased penile blood flow and maybe even death if you make your yohimbine tea a little too strong. Mexican Sage, too, can be smoked or eaten and will also monkey around with your visual perception.

A few Mexican *Turbina corymbosa* plants will provide you with morning glory seeds. These contain the active ingredient d-lysergic acid amide, which is chemically very similar to LSD. *Ipomoea violacea* is another source of morning glory seeds. It crops up in America in a number of different varieties and with a range of different names, including heavenly blue, pearly gates, flying saucers, blue star, summer skies and wedding bells.

Another organic group of hallucinogens is the Solanaceae family. This group includes not only the common potato but also potent and deadly plants such as mandrake, henbane and belladonna. These were reportedly used for centuries by sorcerers and witches for healing and for mystical excursions. Mandrake root, for example, was the vital ingredient in flying potions, with ointment derived from it being rubbed into a receptive mucous membrane, such as the vagina, to produce intense and frequently sexually ecstatic hallucinations. Some authorities have wondered whether women might have used a handy implement such as a broomstick to rub mandrake and henbane into their genitals. If so, this might explain one enduring image of witchcraft.

Ayahuasca, or yage, is another natural hallucinogen widely used in South America. There is not, however, any such thing as an ayahuasca or yage plant. Ayahuasca is the name of an hallucinogenic concoction made from a number of naturally occurring substances which have a psychedelic effect only once they are mixed together. The various shamans who prepare ayahuasca may even all have their own individual recipes. It is believed, though, that the two most popular ingredients are *Banisteriopsis caapi* vine and the leaves of the *Psychotria viridis* bush.

Khat

Another stimulating shrub for you to chew on is khat, or, to give it its proper name, *Catha edulis*. This is a scrawny-leaved, thirsty, seedless plant grown in Ethiopia, the Yemen and Kenya. It reaches about 3–6 metres (10–20 feet) in height and has strong-smelling, glossy crimson-brown leaves, which in time turn leathery, yellowy-green and very smelly. The young shoots near the top of the plant are the best for chewing.

Khat is chewed like tobacco to release its active ingredient cathinone, and its effects are a bit like those of speed, including a mild cocaine-like euphoria but without the rush or the paranoia. And while it's high in a druggy sense, it's also high in vitamin C, which is, of course, more than you can say for heroin. Not only that but it's fresh. It has to be. Khat's cathinone stays active for only 48 hours after picking. So in the US khat tends to be shipped in on Thursdays, Fridays and Saturdays ready for weekend use.

In some parts of East Africa and Arabia khat is still used socially by around 80 per cent of all adults. It hasn't really caught on so much in the West, but it has remained legal in the UK. Around 7 tons of khat pass through Heathrow airport each week and end up openly on sale in London green-grocers for about £4 a bunch.

THERE is anecdotal evidence that khat causes constipation. In the 1950s, when British military authorities banned the use of khat in Aden, a huge reduction in the sale of over-the-counter laxatives followed.

Mushrooms

Closer to home, and potentially making your lawn a lot more colourful, are the many varieties of 'magic' mushroom. Essentially there are two main groups of magic mushroom. One group, including the Liberty Cap mushroom, contains the active ingredients psilocybin and psilocin. The second, smaller, group, which includes the Fly Agaric mushroom, contains ibotenic acid and muscimol.

The Liberty Cap is a small yellow-brown mushroom with a conical cap and which usually grows in long lines. It's popular with magic mushroom enthusiasts because it contains reasonably predictable levels of active chemicals. The problem is – as indeed with any wild mushrooms you might want for perfectly innocent reasons – that there are hundreds of different varieties out there, a lot of them look very similar and a lot of them are very poisonous.

The mushrooms of Fly Agaric's Amanita family are easier to recognise. Unfortunately, though, that's because they include some of the most dangerous fungi in the world, including the invitingly named Death Cap and Destroying Angel. Fly Agaric itself is the red and white spotted toadstool from a thousand children's story book illustrations. It has been suggested that its association with such fairy vistas is because its effects make the world of the little people perceptible to its users. Whether this is true or not, it certainly seems to induce a sense of oneness with nature. Unfortunately, there is a distinct possibility of this becoming a very literal oneness with nature. Fly Agaric is highly poisonous, and around 10 people a year in Europe are killed as a result of eating it.

For Liberty Caps an effective dose is estimated to be about 10 to 30 mushrooms. Large quantities of Liberty Cap are lethal however. As regards the law in Britain, psycho-active mushrooms are legal if they are freshly picked, but they become illegal if you do anything else to them, such as dry them, cook them or set up a small shop in the high street selling them.

 ## Ergot

If you make yourself ill after crawling around woodland filling a punnet with magic mushrooms, at least you should realise what you've done to yourself. With another naturally occur-ring hallucinogen the link was not so clear.

Ergot is a mould that grows on rye and other grasses. The only time it is noticeable is during the winter, when it may be seen as black grains. It was from one of the substances contained in ergot, lysergic acid, that Albert Hoffmann first derived LSD, in 1938. Ergot's effects weren't, however, completely unknown prior to this time. It was used for hundreds of years to help in childbirth, as it constricts the blood vessels in the uterus and can thus prevents haemor-rhaging after delivery.

A lot of people in the past consumed ergot without realising it. During the summer in the Middle Ages, prior to the harvest in August, food reserves would be at their lowest, with barns and grain bins almost empty. So, ironically, while the fields were full

ONE Victorian traveller who investigated the use of Fly Agaric was the mycologist Mordecai Cooke. Cooke was a friend of none other than Charles Dodgson, a.k.a. Lewis Carroll, whose books *Alice in Wonderland* and *Through the Looking Glass* are taken by some as children's fantasies and by others as drug-induced visions. Certainly in *Alice in Wonderland* Alice comes into contact with a series of drug-like substances. There is the caterpilar's hookah pipe, and Alice consumes various bottles of potions and pieces of mushroom that cause her to grow to either vast or very small size. The inability to judge size is said to be one of the effects of Fly Agaric, as is – as we have noted – a feeling of oneness with nature, which may account for Alice's ability to converse with the various animals she meets. Some might also argue that the mushroom's hallucinatory effects can transform the everyday world into a wonderland, albeit a sometimes terrifying one.

of new crops almost ready for harvest, the peasants could be on the point of starvation. This phenomenon was known as 'the hungry gap'. As Robert Lacey and Danny Danziger point out in their book *The Year 1000*, Flemish artist Pieter Breughel the Elder (painting at the end of the Middle Ages) depicted countryfolk in fits of mass hysteria. This was partly due to a lack of solid food and partly because what food they did have left was covered in ergot. As if that wasn't enough, this naturally occurring 'acid' would then have been mixed up with hedgerow herbs and grains, including poppies and hemp, to fill out the peasants' dwindling stocks of flour. The result was what Lacey and Danziger describe as a medieval hash brownie, known to our ancestors as 'crazy bread'.

If all this sounds a bit far out, the phenomenon was observed as recently as 15 August 1951 in Pont-Saint-Esprit in southern France, where 200 people fell ill, three people died and about 50 others became insane after the local farmer, miller and baker turned a blind eye to rye contamination in the village's flour.

The 50 people who suffered insanity had eaten a lot of locally produced bread. They found themselves plagued by horrifying visions, and laughed hysterically, wept, ran mad in the streets, vomited and writhed in agony in their beds. Some felt that they were wrapped inside snakes, one man spent three weeks counting pot lids in his kitchen and another broke out of seven straitjackets and a heavy cowhide belt that had been used to strap him to his bed. He then jumped from a three-storey window and ran half a mile, despite having broken both his legs. He was finally wrestled down and said that he had been in a such hurry because he believed tigers were chasing him.

The medieval name for all this was St Anthony's Fire. The fire was a reference to a terrible sensation of burning in the limbs. This is induced by a constriction of the blood vessels caused by the ergot poisoning, which leads ultimately to gangrene. Sometimes this even caused victims' fingers and toes, or even hands and feet, to fall off. To make matters worse, if you were unlucky enough to suffer ergot poisoning during the Middle Ages, you wouldn't be given medical treatment. Instead, the explanation for the convulsions and hallucinations was simple. It was because you had been possessed.

During the Middle Ages in Europe 40,000 individuals were condemned and executed for witchcraft, and this witch-killing zeal also infected the United States. One famous instance, in Salem, Massachessetts, in 1692, began with several village girls having fits and visions. The story has been told, of course, in Arthur Miller's play, *The Crucible*. Rye has now been shown to have been one of the main crops grown at Salem at the time, and diaries from the period describe the spring of 1692 as having been warm and wet. These are exactly the conditions that favour the development of the ergot mould. Those who suffered fits and visions at Salem also all came from the western side of the village, then adjoining swampy marshlands, where ergot may have flourished.

American scientist Linda Caporael first identified ergot as a possible explanation for the events in Salem from one detail. It wasn't just people who became bewitched, it was also animals, and in Salem in 1692 grain was used to feed livestock as well as people. In the 1951 French outbreak, a dog that had been observed eating scraps of bread went on to run madly in circles, break off its own teeth after gnashing on rocks and finally die. In Salem the court investigating the possession of the village girls fed a 'witch cake' – a piece of bread soaked with the urine of one of the girls – to a dog. The animal duly became bewitched or, as is now believed, poisoned by ergot. Clearly devilish work was afoot. In Salem 150 people were imprisoned and 19 executed, charged with bewitching the girls.

INNOVATIONS

 Advances in science

The 19th and 20th centuries were a period of astounding innovation by scientists, inventors and businessmen throughout Europe and America. Their achievements form the basis of many aspects of life that are taken for granted today. But they didn't just come up with TVs, telephones, computers, cars, aeroplanes and so on. They revolutionised the world of drug-taking as well.

Opium and the many preparations that used opium as a main ingredient were enormous sellers in the Victorian age. It was not until very end of the 19th century, however, that the Bayer chemical company in Germany first marketed the most popular opium-derived product ever produced. It's still on sale just about everywhere and is being used by people all around the world every single day.

Can you guess what it is yet?

The story of Heroin (TM)

The chief pharmacologist at Bayer's factory was a man called Heinrich Dreser. Dreser was in charge of testing new drugs for the company and was highly respected as the most methodical expert in his field, producing the most reliable results. He achieved this at least in part because he was the first person to test drugs on animals on a vast scale. Dreser was so good that his employers paid him a percentage on the profits made from any drugs the company marketed following the results of his tests.

Heinrich Dreser was successful already, but he had his biggest year ever in 1897. It was in this year that his assistant, Felix Hoffmann, presented him with two new chemical compounds. One was acetylsalicylic acid. The other was diacetylmorphine. They were to become the two most successful drugs of the next 100 years.

Acetylsalicyic acid was to be marketed by Bayer under the name aspirin. Dreser came up with an even catchier name for diacetylmorphine. After testing it on frogs, rabbits and sticklebacks, he went on to try it out on the workers at Bayer's factory. They loved the new drug and said it made them feel *heroisch*, or heroic. And that's where Bayer got his snappy name for the new product. Heroin, the heroic or super-strong drug.

So 'heroin' is not a scientific or traditional name for a substance; it's a name invented for a marketed product, like Coca-Cola or Budweiser or Nescafé (to name a few other drug-imbued cash cows). Perhaps, then, we should refer to it as Heroin (TM). There again, Bayer recently held a major celebration on the occasion of aspirin's 100th birthday. There was little celebration by anyone of 100 years of heroin.

Back in 1897, faced with pushing either aspirin or heroin, Dreser was spoilt for choice. But in the end the answer was obvious. Heroin was clearly the drug to go with! As Dreser pointed out, there was obviously not going to be any future for aspirin. Aspirin had an 'enfeebling' action on the heart, he said. Heroin was sure to be the big money-spinner for the Bayer Company.

In fact, although Dreser was to claim otherwise, diacetyl-morphine, a.k.a. heroin, had first been created almost 25 earlier, in 1874, by a chemist called C.R. Alder Wright working at St Mary's Hospital in London.

Wright had been trying to find the essence of morphine. Morphine itself was a derivative of opium that had first been isolated by Frederick William Serturner around 1806. The idea throughout the 19th century had been that if you processed opium to get rid of everything except the pain-relieving

AT the turn of the century heroin was the leading treatment for coughs, catarrh, asthma and bronchitis. The Bayer Company sent out leaflets to physicians promoting, 'Heroin: the Sedative for Coughs ... order a supply from your jobber.' At the time, diseases such as tuberculosis and pneumonia were major causes of death and even routine coughs and colds could create severe problems. Heroin sedated the air passages, depressed respiration and gave the taker a good night's sleep for once. What a godsend!

element, you'd get rid of all the things that made the drug addictive along the way. You'd finally be left with a substance that was not only thoroughly effective but also completely safe and non-addictive. Wrong again!

After C.R. Alder Wright and his colleagues at St Mary's failed to spot the potential of their work, the Bayer Company registered their trademark and launched Heroin (TM) in 1898. It was a huge success. Soon Bayer were exporting to 23 countries a year. By 1902, 5 per cent of all the company's profits were coming from heroin, the fantastic new cure for coughs.

Soon Bayer's product was available in all manner of forms: heroin pastilles, heroin cough lozenges, heroin tablets, water-soluble heroin salts and heroin elixir in a glycerine solution. It wasn't long, though, before doctors began to notice that their patients were getting through an awful lot of cough mixture.

Bayer had marketed safe, non-habit-forming heroin not only as a cough cure but also as a cure for morphine addiction. In the USA the St James Society had campaigned for free samples of heroin that they could give to morphine addicts. Studies at the time were cautious about the new drug. By 1911, however, the truth had emerged. The British Pharmaceutical Codex recognised that heroin was, after all, as addictive as morphine. In 1913 Bayer stopped production.

Felix Hoffmann must have been a plucky lad. Unphased by his boss snubbing his second best discovery, aspirin, he'd carried on working on it himself. Of course, he'd kept this a secret from Dreser. Luckily for the Bayer Company, they were now able to launch aspirin to fill the financial gap created by ceasing heroin production. Luckily for Heinrich Dreser, he now claimed aspirin as his own, despite having initially rejected it. Aspirin went on to sell 40 billion tablets a year. It made Dreser's and Bayer's fortune. Unlike Dreser, Felix Hoffmann was not, as far as we know, on a profit share.

After leaving Bayer, Dreser worked as honorary professor at his own pharmacological institute. Following the death of his wife, he gave up the institute and moved to Zurich, where he remarried. He finally died in 1924 of a stroke. Although no one knew it at the time, the one thing that might have helped this condition was an aspirin tablet taken each day. Dreser wasn't taking aspirin though. It's rumoured that he was still sticking by his first choice. Dreser is alleged to have become addicted to heroin and it is said that this contributed to his decline. Once again, heroin was the wrong drug.

Hillbilly heroin

In the late 1990s deaths began to occur in the USA as a result of use of the prescription painkiller Oxycodone, or Oxycontin. Oxy became renowned as 'Hillbilly heroin' because of its early abuse in the sparsely inhabited area of Appalachia. Subsequently, pharmacies in other parts of the US became subject to armed raids by drug dealers and users in search of supplies of the drug. The Oxy Kills website testifies to the drug's enormous popularity with American youth and describes it as 'heroin in a pill'. Pharmacists likewise have described the drug as being 'as close to heroin as you can get'.

DRUGS | A USER'S GUIDE

Oxycodone is in fact synthesised from an alkaloid of opium called thebaine. Naturally occurring opium contains over a dozen separate alkaloids or psychoactive chemical ingredients. These include not only thebaine but also codeine and morphine. Like morphine and its derivative heroin, Oxy is an extraordinarily strong and highly addictive painkiller.

Oxy, however, does have a legitimate use in the treatment of chronic pain, for which it is highly effective. Oxy pills are thus designed to release their active ingredients into the user's system steadily over a 12-hour period, but if they are chewed, crushed, snorted or broken open for injection, the clever time-release system tends not to work and a high dose is released into the body all in one go. Particularly if used with alcohol or other depressants, Oxy's respiratory depressant effects can very possibly bring your entire cardio-vascular system to a grinding halt.

In Britain the death of 19-year-old aspiring model Samantha Jenkinson was the first to be linked to the drug. Oxycodone was also the drug police accused actress Winona Ryder of being in illegal possession of at the time of her arrest for shoplifting from the Saks Fifth Avenue Store in Beverly Hills. The drugs possession charges against Ryder were however dropped at the request of her prosecutors in October 2002.

Vicodin (Vike to its friends) or hydrodocodone, on the other hand, is a combination of a synthetic narcotic with a non-narcotic painkiller. Again, it is a highly addictive substance now being widely abused in the US. Sonny Bono's widow, Mary, attributed the death of her husband in a skiing accident to the use of Vicodin and other drugs prescribed for chronic back and neck problems. Although Sonny's autopsy found no sign alcohol or drug abuse, Mary claimed he was taking 15 to 20 pills a day, which she believed caused him to become moody and withdrawn, making their marriage 'a very difficult 12 years'. One-time addict, rapper Eminem has a Vike tattoo.

Coke comes alive

In the late 19th century, one scientist was determined to make his name by championing a newly developed wonder drug that he believed could be used to cure a vast array of ailments, including addiction to other drugs. The drug was called cocaine and the scientist's name was Sigmund Freud. Both of them went on to be famous but not for the reasons envisaged at the time.

The substance we now know as cocaine had first been scientifically isolated from coca leaves in 1859 by Albert Nieman, a chemist at Göttingen University. Nieman had soaked the coca in water and lime for three days and added alcohol. Eventually cocaine solids formed out of the mixture. Nieman was given a PhD but died the following year from unknown causes.

Freud got involved in the story because he had fallen in love. He was desperate to marry the love of his life, Martha Bernay. Martha's family, however, hated the idea. If Freud could make some major scientific discovery, the celebrity and money that would come his way would surely change their minds. To date Freud's contribution to the world of science consisted of being the first person to have located eels' genitals. When he began to hear claims of cocaine being used to treat morphine addiction, Sigmund heard wedding bells chime.

In April 1884 Freud acquired a quantity of cocaine. He had a good friend called Ernst von Fleischl-Marxow. Luckily for Sigmund, Ernst was severely addicted to morphine. He was therefore an ideal guinea pig for proving the effectiveness of cocaine in curing addiction. When Ernst von Fleischl-Marxow died in 1891 he was still addicted to morphine. He was also, for good measure, addicted to cocaine. In fact, he would take the two drugs at the same time. Freud may not have discovered a new wonder drug but von Fleischl-Marxow had managed to invent the speed ball. He also discovered coke bugs – the sensation, induced by cocaine poisoning, of insects crawling beneath the skin – and spent much time attempting to pick them out of his flesh.

The early results of Freud's tests had, however, been encouraging. When Sigmund had first given Ernst cocaine, it seemed to swiftly overcome his interest in morphine. So Freud published his paper, 'Über Coca', singing the praises of the new drug and making a wide variety of claims for it, including its ability to cure morphine addiction. 'Über Coca' went to press in July 1884. That's a bare three and a half months since Sigmund had first laid hands on the drug. He must have been desperate to get married.

Cocaine had, nevertheless, clearly made quite an impression on Freud. His biographer Ernest Jones notes that in 'Über Coca' Sigmund seems particularly enthusiastic about his subject. Jones describes how Freud refers to his work as 'a song of praise', while using expressions 'uncommon in a scientific paper', including 'the most gorgeous excitement' that animals display after being given cocaine. Freud also referred to giving patients an 'offering' rather than a dose of cocaine. Sigmund had, as you may have guessed, tried cocaine himself, on 30 April. He was so impressed that he posted a sample to his fiancée, Martha, to help make her strong and to make her cheeks red. The following year he wrote to warn her off the drug.

By 1885 it was becoming clear that cocaine was not as non-addictive as Sigmund might have first led us to believe. A year after being introduced to the drug, Ernst von Fleischl-Marxow was getting through around 1,800 marks' worth of cocaine every few months and was injecting himself with a gram of the substance each day. One gram of cocaine has, in recent years, been estimated as the lethal quantity for a normal adult. The sad truth at last dawned on Sigmund. Ernst was obviously the sort of person who would get addicted to anything.

Ernst was, as Freud described him, exceptional in his craving and he, like all the other people who had become addicted to cocaine, had done so only because they had already been morphine addicts and were clearly weak in will power. The other thing Ernst had done wrong was to take cocaine intravenously rather than orally, as Freud had advised. Injecting cocaine was another thing that caused addiction, claimed Sigmund.

By 1885 von Fleischl-Marxow was in such a bad way that his good friend Sigmund hoped he would die soon, as clearly his body was unable to withstand much more. Dr Freud's diagnosis was wrong once again. Ernst survived for another six addicted years. Someone, nevertheless, benefited from the whole sorry business. Thanks to the publicity Freud had whipped up, the Merck chemical company's production of cocaine had increased from 0.4 kilograms a year in 1883 to 83,343 kilograms in 1885.

Freud also went on using cocaine himself, as it helped make him more talkative. It particularly helped as he tried to ingratiate himself with Jean-Martin Charcot, the celebrated French professor neurologist who inspired Sigmund to move into the study of neuroses and ultimately to develop psycho-analysis. Sigmund also continued to use cocaine to cheer himself up in the absence of his fiancée, Martha, whom he eventually married in September 1886. It's nice when these stories have a happy ending, isn't it?

Speeding in

In 1887 a Japanese scientist, Dr Nagoyoshi Nagai, isolated ephedrine, the active ingredient of the ephedra plant, and in 1893 he synthesised methamphetamine from ephedrine. In 1927 Gordon Alles, an American researcher, synthesised amphetamine. An ephedrine substitute could now be made cheaply and artificially without the need for plant materials to be brought into the USA from the Far East. It was this synthetic amphetamine that was put into the Benzedrine inhaler to treat asthma and hay fever. It was also used in the treatment of depression, narcolepsy, Parkinson's Disease and epilepsy. Unexpectedly, in view of its effect of speeding people up, it also turned out to be useful in making hyper-active children more manageable.

By 1958, 3.5 billion tablets were being produced in the USA annually, rising to 10 billion in 1970. Other varieties of amphetamine that were developed included dexamphetamine, which was marketed as Dexedrine (Dexies) and which was twice as strong as Benzedrine (Bennies); and methylamphetamine, marketed as Methedrine or Desoxyn, which was twice the strength of Dexedrine. Another variety was phenmetrazine, which was marketed as Preludin. It was 'Prellies' that famously enabled the Beatles to perform eight-hour-long shows in the bars of Hamburg during their residence there in 1961.

 ## It's methylenedioxymethamphetamine time!

During the 20th century, scientists working at the world's pharmaceutical companies seemed to be turning out new types of drugs in industrial quantities. These substances were apparently patented en masse before the process of establishing just what they could be used for even began.

In the 1950s Gordon Alles, the scientist who had synthesised amphetamine, did some research on one such drug, the catchily titled methylenedioxymethamphetamine, or MDMA. MDMA had in fact first been synthesised way back in 1912 by the German pharmaceutical company Merck, which had done so well with cocaine a couple of decades earlier. Alles described the drug's effects of heightening perception and producing visual distortions. As research continued in the 1960s, MDMA was given the pet name Adam because of its supposed effects of releasing the user's innocent 'inner child'. The name Adam failed to catch on. Instead the drug became rather more famous a few decades later, by which time it had acquired the street name ecstasy.

MDMA research was carried on in the 1960s by another American scientist, Alexander Shulgin. After serving in the US Navy during World War Two and going on to study chemistry, Shulgin joined the staff of the Dole Chemical Company. In 1960, shortly before taking the job at Dole, Shulgin had tried mescaline. Finding this a life-changing experience, he went on to take a great interest in other drugs that had similar effects. His employees at Dole noticed that Shulgin had a highly individual method of testing drugs. Instead of testing them on animals, Shulgin seemed much keener on the idea of taking them himself to analyse their effects. This technique was regarded as somewhat dubious by the conservative Dole company and, in 1966, Shulgin left to work in his own home laboratory.

Shulgin had synthesised MDMA while at Dole and then carried on working on it at home. In the 1970s he began promoting the drug for use in therapy sessions. MDMA was used to help terminally ill patients deal with their illness and also proved particularly useful in marriage guidance counselling. After a supervised dose even couples carrying years of grudges and resentment were able to see one another's point of view. If only this therapeutic use of the drug had been developed to its next logical stage: international peace negotiations.

INNOVATIONS

SOME other scientists who got themselves into trouble were a group researching the drug thebaine at the Edinburgh laboratories of MacFarlan, Smith & Co during the 1960s. Thanks to their work, the drug etorphine was developed. Unfortunately, before they realised just what they'd come up with, the scientists all decided to have a nice cup of tea. In the absence of a spoon or even a biro, they stirred their refreshing drinks using a glass rod that had recently been used in their experiments. It was some time before they regained consciousness and realised the potency of the substance they had developed. Etorphine is 10,000 times as powerful as morphine and is used to knock out elephants and rhinos.

Because he had helped the American Drug Enforcement Administration over the years as a consultant and expert witness, Shulgin had been given a special licence to carry on his research into psychoactive drugs. This, of course, often involved not only research but the invention of brand-new drugs. Working in his lab, Shulgin turned out a series of chemical creations using oils from substances like nutmeg, sassafras, crocus and saffron as starting points. The result was that on more than one occasion the DEA brought Shulgin drugs that had been found circulating on the street only to have him identify them as something he had recently invented himself in his back room. After a raid on his house in 1994, Shulgin's DEA licence was revoked and the professor was given a hefty fine to boot.

Technicolour

It may have inspired popular music a generation before ecstasy, but LSD is actually the younger drug. It emerged from the work of scientists at the pharmaceutical company Sandoz at Basle in Switzerland. Dr Arthur Stoll first isolated the active ingredient in the grain mould ergot in 1918. Then, carrying on Stoll's research, his assistant Albert Hoffmann worked throughout the 1920s to synthesise compounds related to ergot and explore their use in relation to migraine, obstetrics and geriatrics.

In 1938 Sandoz decided that Hoffman's work was getting nowhere and it was suspended. In April 1943, however, Hoffman got the chance to synthesise the last in the series of 25 chemicals he had developed: d-lysergic acid diethylamide 25, or LSD-25.

LSD-25 involved mixing lysergic acid derived from the ergot mould with diethylamide. The mixture was then frozen and the results distilled or evaporated. Tests on animals seemed to suggest that the substance didn't have much effect. But then Hoffmann accidentally got some on his fingers. A nibble on his fingernails later, Albert began to get an inkling of what he'd come up with. The lesson for the rest of us is: never trust a scientist to make you a sandwich.

On 19 April 1943, following his accidental ingestion of the drug, Hoffman purposefully gave himself a dose of one-thousandth of a gram of LSD diluted in 10cc of water. Within 40 minutes he was unable to string two sentences together. So he decided to go for a bike ride. Hoffmann asked his assistant to accompany him as he cycled home.

'I lost all account of time,' related Hoffmann. 'I noticed with dismay that my environment was undergoing progressive changes. My visual field wavered and everything appeared deformed as if in a faulty mirror. I was overcome with fear that I was going out of my mind. Occasionally I felt as if I were out of my body. I thought I had died. My ego seemed suspended somewhere in space from where I saw my dead body lying on the sofa. It was particularly striking how acoustic perceptions such as the noise of water gushing from a tap or the spoken word were transformed into optical illusions.'

After a doctor had diagnosed that he was physically sound, Hoffman began to relax. 'Now, little by little, I could begin to enjoy the unprecedented colours and plays of shapes ... Kaleidoscopic, fantastic images surged in on me, alternating, variegated, opening and then closing themselves in circles and spirals, exploding in coloured fountains, rearranging and hybridising themselves in constant flux.'

In neutral Switzerland, in the centre of Europe in the middle of World War Two, the drug of peace and love had been discovered.

While cocaine had been championed by the father of psychoanalysis and ecstasy by a renegade chemist, the first disciple to spread the word of LSD was a British cultural attaché based in New York, Michael Hollingshead. After hearing of LSD from the novelist Aldous Huxley, Hollingshead got a doctor friend to write out an order on a sheet of New York hospital letterheaded paper claiming that it was needed 'as a "control" drug for a series of bone-marrow experiments'. A few days later Hollingshead received a package from the Sandoz company containing 'Lot no. H-00047', a batch of pharmaceutical LSD sufficient for 5,000 doses, together with a bill for $285.

Hollingshead noted that the substance resembled malted milk powder. He mixed it into a stiff paste with water and icing sugar and then spooned the mixture back into a 16-ounce mayonnaise jar. According to Hollingshead the mayonnaise jar contained 5,000 spoonfuls, each therefore sufficient to provide an eight-hour LSD trip. Hollingshead had, however, consumed several doses while decanting the mixture into the jar.

Hollingshead's mayonnaise jar became legendary and was regularly produced at parties at his apartment. Among those turned on to the drug at these soirées was a professor of psychiatry from Harvard University, Dr Timothy Leary.

Apparently suffering a mid-life crisis after the suicide of his first wife and the failure of his second marriage, Leary had tried psilocybin mushrooms during a break in Mexico. Leary was so impressed by the effects that he established a psilocybin research project at Harvard. He was then converted to the use of LSD, which he set out to promote with religious zeal. Harvard sacked Leary on grounds of holding orgies, but subsequently William Mellon Hitchcock, a 20-year-old millionaire stockbroker, came to his financial rescue. Hitchcock funded Leary to establish the Castalia Foundation in a mansion in upstate New York to promote the use of LSD. Similarly, Michael Hollingshead acted as Leary's agent in London, founding the World Psychedelic Centre in the King's Road.

In the words of www.leary.com, Leary was 'a philosopher and a scientist, whose underlying motivations were human communication and understanding the mind'. He spent his adult life working 'to enliven the human spirit and raise the level of social consciousness' and recognised psychedelic drugs as having potentially great positive results, including, for example, the 'curing' of convicted criminals. During the 1960s, as LSD gained in popularity, Leary became recognised as its guru. His prominent role in the counter-culture led ultimately to his imprisonment on drugs offences, escape, recapture and eventual release in 1976.

However bizarre or ridiculous he may have seemed on occasion, Leary was absolutely sincere in his promotion of LSD as a means of revelation to mankind and in his belief that 'drugs are the religion of the 21st century'. He was also perhaps more reverential with regard to LSD's effects than many of the followers who heeded his advice to 'turn on, tune in and drop out'. Leary was, however, declared 'the most dangerous man in America' by no less an authority on the subject than President Richard Nixon. Coincidentally, in 1982 Leary went on a lecture tour across the USA in league with G. Gordon Liddy. Liddy was not only renowned as a Watergate villain but had, in 1966, as district attorney of

'TAKING LSD is a bit like visiting Stratford-upon-Avon. It's quite nice but once you've been there you don't really feel the need to ever go back again.'

– John Peel

MOTHER'S LITTLE HELPERS – popular tranquillisers of the post-war era

Librium (Chlorodiazepoxide) Launched in 1960 as a treatment for anxiety and insomnia by the Hoffman-La Roche chemical company following trials at the University of Texas a year earlier. Tests had included giving the drug to zoo animals including a lion who was filmed quite literally lying down with a lamb. Librium was the first in a new line of tranquilliser pills based around benzodiazepine chemicals. These new drugs were introduced as a safe, non-addictive alternative to barbiturates. Early research by Dr Leo Hollister began to show that the truth was somewhat different and benzodiazepine users did develop dependence and suffer withdrawal symptoms.

Valium (Diazepam) Stronger than Librium, and another hugely famous benzodiazepine tranquilliser. Developed by Dr Leo Sternbach of Hoffman-La Roche, Valium first became available over the counter in 1963. Like Librium it is a hypnotic tranquilliser the effects of which last around twelve hours and which provides either relaxation, Dutch courage or a sense of reckless invincibility to its various classes of users. Because of its long-acting nature it can lead to fatigue if taken during the day or a hangover if taken overnight. Strongly associated with the figure of the 'housewife junkie', prescriptions for Valium and other benzodiazepines were clocking up worldwide sales of $1,000,000,000 by the mid-1970s.

Temazepam (Temazepam) Yet another from the many benzodiazepine tranquillisers launched over the years. Temazepam was marketed specifically for insomnia but became particularly popular as a recreational drug. The attempt by some to inject Temazepam from capsules

Dutchess County directed a raid on Leary's Millbrook commune.

When he developed inoperable prostate cancer Leary planned an elaborate ritual to be broadcast live on the internet which would involve his ending of his own life. He died before this idea came to fruition but took drugs to the end while continuing to advise the world to question authority. Following his death in 1996, a portion of Leary's cremated remains, along with those of *Star Trek* creator Gene Roddenberry, were launched on a rocket from the Canary Islands to a final resting place in space.

that had been treated to make it uninjectable resulted in gangrene and a variety of lost body parts from toes to limbs.

Quaaludes (Methaqualone) Methaqualone was first synthesised in India in 1955 by M. L. Gujral and marketed in the UK in the mid-1960s with an antihistamine under the name Mandrax and then in the United States as Quaaludes. Originally designed as a sleeping pill but taken while awake they produced a drunken serenity. 'Mandies' or 'Ludes' thus became popular recreational drugs in the 1970s and were even name-checked in David Bowie's song 'Rebel Rebel' ('You've got your transmission and your live wire/ You got your cue line and a handful of ludes.')

Other brand names: Ativan (Lorazepam), Dalmane (Flurazepam), Dormonoct (Loprazolam) Frisium (Clobazam), Halcion (Triazolam), Hypnovel (Midazolam), Lexotan (Bromazepam) Mogadon (Nitrazepam), Noctamid (Lormetazepam), Rohypnol (Flunitrazepam), Serenid D (Oxazepam), Tranxene (Clorazepate), Xanax (Alprazolam)

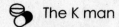 The K man

PCP was first synthesised in 1926 and was marketed as an anaesthetic under the name of Sernyl from the 1950s. The 1971 *IT Book of Drugs* described PCP as 'a strong animal tranquiliser' that was sprayed onto parsley, mint or grass, hence the Angel Dust nickname. *IT* described it as 'not a good drug'. In 1962 a derivative of PCP was developed and began to be used as an anaesthetic for animals and, in some cases, for humans. This was ketamine.

The American psychiatrist John Lilly experimented with LSD and later ketamine, regarding ketamine as 'a quantum transporter' to another universe. In interviews Lilly was, perhaps sensibly, shy about publicising his use of ketamine and referred to it obliquely as vitamin K. Among his other projects, Lilly also developed the isolation flotation tank and attempted to communicate with dolphins using computers to translate messages between the species. He took ketamine every day for 100 days, even trying it while inside his flotation tank. The effects were not hallucinations as far as he was concerned; they were other realities or, as in the film based on his experiences, 'altered states'.

Once in these other realities, Lilly, like the shamans of ancient tribes, made contact with the people he found there. In particular he claimed to have made repeated contact with extraterrestrials who informed him that they had removed DNA samples from Earth and transported them to another planet. There, they had genetically engineered all of Earth's large-brained mammals including primates, dolphins and whales before putting them back, fully evolved, on Earth.

Cracking up

It was scientists of a more amateur persuasion who, during the 1970s, contributed to a significant development in the history of Sigmund's favourite, cocaine.

One thing that you can't normally do with cocaine hydrochloride powder is smoke it. It just burns away. Nevertheless, with a little bit of chemical know-how, a method was developed to remove the hydrochloride molecule from cocaine. By adding a strong alkali and dissolving the result in ether or some other powerful solvent, the 'base' of the drug could be crystallised out or 'freed' into a form that could be smoked through a water pipe. The rush from this 'freebase cocaine' was quick and intense, and the substance was much more addictive than powdered cocaine.

In the 1970s freebasing cocaine became hugely popular. At first the method of preparing freebase was a closely guarded secret. Those who had the knack used it to gain access to parties with the great and the good from the worlds of rock music and/or drug trafficking. Soon, though, the secret was out and hundreds of thousands of instruction books and freebase kits were being sold.

Then an even simpler technique for producing smokable cocaine was developed. This involved dissolving cocaine powder in a solution of water and baking soda and letting all this dry out to produce rocks of pure smokable coke. On

17 November 1985 the *New York Times* printed the name of this new type of cocaine for the first time: crack.

Often smoked from pipes or devices made from soft drink cans, crack can also be be mixed with tobacco and/or cannabis in a joint or burned on a piece of tin foil. The reason it's so popular is because, like freebase, it gives a very strong, extraordinarily quick high. You might think snorting cocaine powder gets the mixture inside you in a hurry, but crack gets 80 per cent pure cocaine vapour inside your brain in less than eight seconds. People are in such a hurry these days.

The short duration of the effects of crack means that while it appears cheap in comparison to cocaine powder, a series of rocks have to be taken to stay high just for the duration of an afternoon. Also, apparently as a result of the fact that crack doesn't involve injection, it was a drug that appealed to women. The knock-on effect of all this has been repeated newspaper scare stories about the desperate behaviour of crack addicts and even the phenomenon of crack babies.

Chicago paediatrician Ira Chasnoff made a study of babies born to a number of crack-using mothers. At first it was thought that the 'crack babies' were possibly going to be doomed to a handicapped life because of their mothers' continued smoking of cocaine. In fact, a two-year follow-up study showed them to be normal. Chasnoff reported: 'They are no different from other children growing up. They are not the retarded imbeciles people talk about.' Analysis of the infants born to crack-addicted women showed that most of their problems arose not directly from their mothers' drug habits but from the poverty they were brought up in. It was

'CRACK. Only in New York would a guy invent crack. Only in New York
would there be a guy that cocaine wasn't good enough for.'

– Denis Leary

also noted that the drugged-up mothers were not as diligent
as they might have been in caring for their children.

Crack is of course an extremely dangerous drug. Claims
that it can be instantaneously addictive, however, seem dubious. Stuart Walton, in his book *Out of It*, quotes journalist Ian
Penman's assertion that everyone he knew had tried crack
but no one he knew had become hooked. Another drug user
interviewed by Walton described the effects:

*'For a moment, nothing happens, and then you feel this
great wave of massive, totally unhandleable energy
rolling through you, until you can't actually contain it,
and it's about to burst through your finger-ends, and you
know you won't ever do this again. Then you let out your
breath and you feel so beautiful. For about 10 minutes
you feel like a king. And then you want to do it again.'*

'And did you?'

'I did it once more, and I've never touched it since.'

 Cake

Somehow civilisation has so far survived crack, heroin and all
the other chemical innovations of the last hundred years or
so. The 20th century did, however, have one final drugs

GREAT PERFORMANCE-ENHANCING DRUGS SCANDALS:

1876 The first doping scandal during a 24-hour walking race at the Agricultural Hall, Islington. The competitors were an Englishman, who gave up after 14 hours, and an American, who kept going for 24 hours and covered 109.5 miles. It turned out that he had been chewing coca leaves throughout the race. Despite an outcry he was not stripped of his title.

1904 Olympic marathon runner Thomas Hicks almost died after taking brandy and strychnine.

1960 Danish Olympic cyclist Kurt Jensen died after taking amphetamines.

1988 Olympic sprinter Ben Johnson tested positive for anabolic steroids and was stripped of his gold medal.

menace up its arm, more terrible than any that had gone before. And it came courtesy not of a scientist but of a comedian. In 1997 Christopher Morris's classic TV show *Brass Eye* showed just how quickly public figures would leap onto any new drugs bandwagon, regardless of the facts.

The subject of the programme was a new drugs menace, cake. Cake, according to Morris, was 'a bisturbile cranabolic amphetamoid' which 'affects the part of the brain that deals with time perception – known as "Shatner's Bassoon"'. Cake was such a terrible substance that it caused one boy to become so ill he coughed up his own pelvis.

Not suspecting it was a set-up, luminaries such as Bernard

Manning lent their services to record messages to warn young people about cake. 'Some little kiddie cried all the water out of his body,' intoned the comedian to camera. 'How do you think his mother felt? It's a f***ing disgrace.'

Cake was, of course, as *Brass Eye* punningly pointed out, 'a made-up drug'. As well as Bernard Manning, however, MPs Sir Graham Bright and David Amess also both agreed to make contributions to the programme, believing it to be a serious investigation into a real drug. Questions about 'the drug, cake' ended up being asked in the House of Commons.

The Independent Television Commission upheld the MPs' complaints that they had been unaware of the nature of the programme to which they had been invited to contribute. The ITC did, however, at least recognise that the 'legitimate targets of the satire ... were media treatments of subjects such as drug-taking and the role of public figures'.

New drugs may indeed prove to be a menace, but then so is hysteria and misinformation.

MARKETING OPPORTUNITIES

*'Junk is the ideal product ... the ultimate merchandise.
No sales talk necessary. The client will crawl through a
sewer and beg to buy ... The junk merchant ...
degrades and simplifies the client.'*

– William S. Burroughs

 ## The drugs business

Drugs are big business. They are, however, big criminal business. Although the drugs industry generates vast amounts of money, by definition all of these funds go to criminals. It wasn't always like this. It was only in the early 20th century that recreational drugs were made illegal. Before this even what are now known to be the hardest drugs were on general sale in high streets across Britain and America. Sometimes they were sold neat. Sometimes they were the active ingredient in any one of an unending range of medicines, tonics and pick-me-ups. Some of these, with perhaps a little modification, remain on sale today.

Neat opium

As historian Virginia Berridge points out, Karl Marx was wrong when he said that religion was the opium of the people. The opium of the people in the 19th century was opium. In Britain there were no barriers of any kind to the import, wholesale and retailing of opium until 1868.

Opium was bought by pharmacists or shopkeepers in one-pound blocks wrapped in red paper labelled 'Opium (Turc)'. It was then pounded in a mortar with some honey and made into quarter- or half-ounce loaves. Once wrapped in red waxed paper, it was ready to be put on sale. And sell it did. During the 19th century opium was as commonly used as aspirin 100 years later. It is probable that every British individual alive during the 19th century took opium on at least one occasion during their lives.

Laudanum

Laudanum was one of the most popular forms in which people took opium during the 18th and 19th centuries. Laudanum was developed by the English physician, Thomas Sydenham. Sydenham was known as nothing less than 'the Shakespeare of medicine' and was renowned for

SYDENHAM'S recipe for laudanum

2 ounces of opium

1 ounce of saffron

Dissolve in a pint of Canary or sherry wine

Mix with a drachm of cinnamon powder and cloves powder

Leave in a vapour bath for two to three days

his expertise in cordials. In the 1660s he came up with a new cordial recipe and named it laudanum.

Laudanum caught on in a big way. Throughout the 18th and 19th centuries this was the form in which opium was taken by poets and writers such as Samuel Taylor Coleridge, Thomas De Quincey, John Keats, Sir Walter Scott, Wilkie Collins and Elizabeth Barrett Browning. And these were, of course, just some of the most famous users with the most notable habits.

Dover's Powder

In the early 18th century, Thomas Dover was a pirate leading raids on the South American coast from his ship *The Duke*. On 2 February 1709, Dover and his men rescued a ship-wrecked sailor called Alexander Selkirk from the Juan Fernandez Islands. A few years later, Selkirk was the inspiration for Daniel Defoe's 1719 work, *The Life and Strange*

Surprising Adventures of Robinson Crusoe. On his return to England, Dover made a perhaps surprising change of career. He set up in medical practice and created a patent remedy that was so popular it was still on sale at the outbreak of World War Two.

Dover's Powder was marketed principally as a treatment for gout and was to be the most widely used such remedy on sale for the next 150 years. Dover's skill in devising the mixture derived from when, as a young man, he had been treated for smallpox by Thomas Sydenham. Impressed at Sydenham's saving his life, Dover learnt medicine from him. You'll never guess what the active ingredient in Dover's Powder was. Sir Thomas Browne detailed the recipe in his *Hydriotaphia*:

> *Take Opium one ounce, Salt-Petre and Tartar vitriolated each four ounces, Ipocacuana one ounce. Put the Salt-Petre and Tartar into a red-hot mortar, stirring them with a spoon until they have done flaming. Then powder them very fine; after that slice in your opium, grind them to a powder, and then mix the other powders with these. Dose from forty to sixty or seventy grains in a glass of white wine Posset going to bed; covering up warm and drinking a quart or three pints of the Posset Drink while sweating.*

Browne also noted that 'Some apothecaries have desired their patients to make their wills and settle their affairs before they venture upon so large a dose as from forty to seventy grains.'

Other Victorian opium concoctions

Dover's Powder was hugely successful but it was only one of many opium products on sale in the 18th and 19th centuries. Dr John Collis Browne's Chlorodyne is another successful product of the Victorian era that survives to this day. Today, though, it no longer contains its original ingredients, which included two grains of morphine per fluid ounce added to chloroform and tincture of cannabis.

Opium was available in pills; lozenges; compound powder of opium, soap and opium; lead and opium pills; vinegar of opium; wine of opium; opium liniment; and opium enema. Opium was also a prominent active ingredient in drinks such as poppyhead tea, as enjoyed in the East Anglian Fen country, sleepy beer and nepenthe. Among patent medicine preparations containing opium were Owbridge's Lung Tonic, Battley's sedative solution and Kendal Black Drop, a substance used by Coleridge and reputed to be four times the strength of laudanum.

Children's opiates

Another area of top-selling opium brands included Mrs Winslow's Soothing Syrup, Dalby's Carminative, Atkinson's

 LONDON theatres used to offer their clientele nitrous oxide or laughing gas to get them in the mood to watch the comedy on stage.

Infant Preservative, Street's Infants Quietness and Godfrey's Cordial, which was sold in elegantly designed steeple-shaped bottles. Yes, the Victorians did not keep their children under control just by rigid discipline. To make sure they were seen but not heard, the kiddies were also given regular doses of class A drugs.

Opium and opium products were also a factor, perhaps inadvertently and perhaps not, in the early demise of many unwanted children. Twins and illegitimate children, it was said, almost always died.

Opium's rival

Towards the end of the 19th century opium had a rival. By 1900 cocaine was in the top five pharmaceutical products in the US and was selling for around $2.50 per gram. Like opium, cocaine was used in a range of different products including cocaine syrups, pastilles, wines, tonics, elixirs, balms, ointments and cordials. Many products contained very high percentages of cocaine indeed. In fact some manufacturers could not have increased the amount of cocaine in their products if they had tried. Rayno's Hay Fever remedy (for hay fever, nose cold, influenza and whenever the nose is 'stuffed up, red and sore') was in fact a pure solution of cocaine. It was recommended that Rayno's preparation be taken 'two to ten times a day'. No wonder patients' noses were 'stuffed up, red and sore'.

Another product, containing a mere 420 milligrams of cocaine per ounce, was Dr Tucker's Asthma Specific which, it was advised, should be applied to the nasal membrane. Ax-ma-syde, Nyall's Compound of Damiana and Paine's Celery Compound also contained coca as their active ingredient. Cocaine impregnated plasters were available as were haemorrhoid creams. The British Pharmaceutical Codex in 1911 detailed the following recipe for piles:

> *Unguentum Gallae and Unguentum Gallae cum Opio are valuable astringents for use in painful haemorrhoids. For similar use, suppositories are prepared containing 3 decigrams (5 grains) of powdered galls with or without 6 centigrams (1 grain) of powdered opium, or 3 centigrams ($\frac{1}{2}$ grain) of cocaine. It should be remembered that the opium has no peripheral action; its whole benefit results from its action on the central nervous system after absorption. Preparations of galls are incompatible with the salts of iron, lead, copper, or silver.*

In 1910 Captain Scott took cocaine and zinc tablets to help him in his expedition to the South Pole. A year earlier Ernest Shackleton had used Forced March cocaine tablets during his Antarctic expedition. Despite not having eaten for 40 hours and being sunburned, frostbitten and exhausted, Shackleton's men were kept going by hourly doses of Forced March, which the manufacturer had advertised as 'capable of sustaining strength without a subsequent depression'. As a result Shackleton's team reached their next depot, and survived.

Cocaine was also used in toothache preparations. One ad from 1885 proffers an instantaneous cure sold by the Lloyd Manufacturing Co. This cocaine preparation for sale by all druggists price 15 cents was advertised with a portrait of a cute little boy and girl in lovely hats building a tiny playhouse out of sticks. The American drug company Parke Davis went so far as to market a cocaine-injecting kit, comprising a syringe, some cocaine powder and a solution to dissolve it in. In Britain during World War One two highly esteemed retail businesses, Harrods and Savory and Moore, were each fined for selling morphine and cocaine in handy packs, ready to be sent off as a special gift for 'friends at the front'.

 ## Tonic wine

Another hugely popular product of the period was Vin Mariani. This tonic wine was the creation of a Corsican pharmacist, Angelo Mariani, who had come to Paris in 1860 to make his fortune. There he saw a report by Paolo Mantegazza about his experience of taking coca during a visit to Peru. Mantegazza declared that coca was useful for treatment of 'a furred tongue in the morning, flatulence, [and] whitening the teeth'.

'God is unjust,' declared Mantegazza, 'because he made man incapable of sustaining the effects of coca all life long. I would rather live a life of 10 years with coca than one of 100,000 (and here I inserted a line of zeros) without it.' Although he was 'by nature extremely unsuited to any sort of gymnastic exercise', the coca made Mantegazza feel like leaping onto a high writing desk and 'jumping on my neighbours' heads'.

Laudanum disguised the bitter taste of opium and was more socially acceptable to European consumers because the drug was dissolved in wine. Vin Mariani performed a similar function for coca. The 'secret' recipe for the product involved little more than steeping ground coca leaves in wine for a few hours and then draining the wine off and bottling it ready for sale.

The recipe for Vin Mariani was not, however, its creator's only innovation. It is rumoured today that cocaine is popular with certain people working in the entertainment industry. If this is the case it all dates right back to Angelo Mariani himself, for in order to market his drink Mariani virtually invented the idea of celebrity product endorsement.

Cases of Vin Mariani were sent to many celebrities of the day. In return for the wine, they were asked for two things: their thoughts on the product and a signed photograph. They seemed, without exception, to have been extremely impressed by the effects of Vin Mariani. The photos and comments flooded back to Mariani, who published them in newspapers, leaflets and even in albums of portraits.

Louis Bleriot said he took Vin Mariani with him when he flew the first solo flight across the English Channel in 1909 ('It was a great help. Its energetic action sustained me during the crossing'). Auguste Bartholdi wished he had had some to hand when he had been constructing the Statue of Liberty ('had I taken it 20 years ago, the Statue of Liberty would have attained the height of several hundred metres'). And novelist

H.G. Wells sent two cartoon portaits of himself: the 'before' picture showed him slouched and run down, and the 'after' showed him raring to go. Vin Mariani was also recommended by Thomas Edison, cinema pioneers the Lumiere brothers, playwright Henrik Ibsen, no less than six Presidents of France, the President of Argentina and the President of the USA, William McKinley, who stated that he was already 'well acquainted' with the product at the time his complimentary sample arrived.

 ## Quite literally, it's coke

Vin Mariani spawned many imitations. One non-alcoholic variation on the idea is still on sale today. You might just have heard of it. What's more, the most famous soft drink in the world remains rich in coca goodness to this day.

In 1884 John Styth Pemberton, a druggist in Georgia, USA, marketed a product he said was even better than Vin Mariani: Pemberton's French Wine Coca. Pemberton claimed his drink was 'a wonderful and delightful remedy'. It was 'infallible in curing all who are afflicted with nerve trouble, dyspepsia, mental and physical exhaustion, all chronic and wasting diseases, gastric irritability, constipation, sick headache, neuralgia ...' while its active ingredient, coca, 'is a most wonderful invigorator of the sexual organs and will cure seminal weakness, impotency etc.'.

Pemberton's Wine Coca was indeed very stimulating, containing not only coca but also caffeine-rich kola nuts. When the spectre of temperance campaigners threatened to reduce the profits from his product, Pemberton came up with an alcohol-free version. Coca-Cola went on sale in 1886, just before Pemberton's home town of Atlanta imposed alcohol prohibition.

Pemberton had come up with the recipe in May that year, disguising the bitter taste of the caffeine and the coca not with wine but with lots of sugar. His marketing team for the new drink included Ed Holland, an old business colleague, and two men who had tried to sell him a printing device a couple of month earlier, Frank Robinson and David Roe. Robinson came up with the writing style on the bottle label and placed an ad in the *Atlanta Daily Journal* on 29 May 1886 announcing 'Coca-Cola, Delicious! Refreshing! Invigorating!'

Coca-Cola sold well at first but then, like many of Pemberton's earlier business ventures, it began to fail. Pemberton had first been interested in coca because many medical authorities at the time had advocated it to help over-come morphine addiction. And Pemberton himself was a morphine addict. Pemberton's addiction dated back to when he was wounded in the civil war. By the time Coca-Cola was launched he was probably not only still addicted to morphine but to cocaine as well.

Pemberton cheated Robinson out of his interest in the product and then sold out his own interests. When added up, the total of the interests sold by Pemberton came to more than 100 per cent of the whole. Robinson consulted his lawyer, who advised him he had a good case but little chance of success. In the end, Robinson's lawyer's brother bought up all outstanding interests in Coca-Cola and Robinson went

OTHER 19th-century cola drinks marketed following the success of Coca-Cola:

Cafe Coca

Celery Cola

Coca Bola

Cola Coca

Dope Cola

Dr Don's Coca

Dr Sampson's Coca Spirits

Inca Cola

Kola Ade

Kola Cordial

Kos Kola

Kumfort's Cola Extract

Lambert Company's Wine of Coca with Peptonate Iron

Liebig's Coca Beef Tonic (just what the world needed – fizzy Bovril)

Maltine's Coca Wine

Metcalf's Coca Wine

Nicol's Compound

Pillsbury's Coke Extract

Quina-Coca

Rococola

Sutcliff and Case Company's Beef, Wine and Coca

Vani Cola

Velo Cola

Vin de Coca de Perou

to work for him. After an initial investment of $2,300, Robinson's lawyer's brother did pretty well out of Coca-Cola. Asa Griggs Candler died 38 years later worth $50 million.

Although alcohol-free and thus a temperence beverage, Coca-Cola did of course provide a double drugs hit of cocaine and caffeine. When, in the early 1900s, talk began in the USA of prohibiting cocaine, a cocaine-free version of Coca-Cola replaced the original recipe. In 1903 the Schaeffer Alkaloidal Works were awarded the contract to remove the cocaine from the coca used in the drink. To this day the company, now called Stepan Chemicals, imports around 175,000 kilograms (385,800 pounds) of truxillense coca a year from Bolivia and Peru. Stepan take delivery of what they euphemistically call 'merchandise number 5' at their plant in Maywood, New Jersey, and there, under armed guard, chemically prepare the coca leaves to make them cocaine-free and ready for use in the Coca-Cola recipe.

The 1.75 tons of cocaine by-product, with an estimated street value of around $200 million, removed by Stepan each year, is presumably either disposed of harmlessly, or used for medical research or as a surgical anaesthetic. A completely coca-free Coca-Cola was launched in the mid-1980s but was a commercial disaster. It was soon replaced by original recipe 'classic Coke'.

If you're thinking that the American government can't have liked Stepan/Coca -Cola importing this amount of coca into the USA, you'd be wrong. Cola's unpublicised imports provided the American Federal Bureau of Narcotics with a very useful foothold and set of contacts to find out what was going on in South America. The sheer value of the business may also have given the USA influence over certain South American goverments.

So Stepan/Coca-Cola were allowed to carry on importing coca and benefited from clauses in international narcotics legislation. For example, clause 27 of the 1961 Convention of the Nations Joined on Narcotics permitted 'the perfuming extract production from the cocaine leaf, since that they do not contain alkalis'. So no other soft drink tastes quite the same as Coca-Cola because no one else is allowed to import 'merchandise number 5'.

 ## Bib-Label Lithiated Lemon-Lime Soda

The practice of marketing American soft drinks with active drug ingredients did, however, continue with a concoction called 'Bib-Label Lithiated Lemon-Lime Soda'. This hang-over cure contained not coca or opium but lithium. Lithium is a lightweight metal used in watch batteries, to make molten glass lighter and stronger, to harden concrete quickly and to kill algae. It is also given to people with manic depression to eat. Doctors aren't entirely sure why it works but it does seem to keep patients from outbursts of promiscuity, rage and suicide. Lithium is also given to chronic cocaine users, and it was once a particularly popular ingredient in soft drinks, which often included minerals found in natural springs in their recipes.

Because of its anti-manic depressive ingredient, it was perhaps appropriate that Bib-Label Lithiated Lemon-Lime

CLASSIC Drug Marketing Slogans

Valium 'Reduce psychic tension'

Prozac 'For both restful nights and productive days'

Ritalin 'Go all day without tiring'

Quaaludes 'For any type of insomnia'

Heroin 'The sedative for coughs'

Soda first went on sale in October 1929, a few weeks before the stock market crash. The algae-killing, watch-powering soda went on to considerable success, but – for some reason – the original name didn't catch on. Soon the drink was renamed 7 UP Lithiated Lemon Soda, and then was shortened to just 7 UP in 1936. 7 UP is, however, perhaps not quite as 'up' as it once was, for lithium was removed from the recipe in 1950.

 ## Hard drugs in the 20th century

The 19th century might have been the great age of drug-imbued mass-market products, but pharmaceutical companies in the 20th century nevertheless went on marketing new formulas, only to find they caught on but not in the way that had been intended.

As we have seen, in the 1970s ecstasy, or, as it was known in those more innocent days, methylenedioxymethamphethamine, was found to be a beneficial aid in marriage guidance counselling. Earlier in the century, in 1932, Smith Kline and French first put the Benzedrine inhaler on sale. It was intended as a decongestant nasal inhaler, to be used by people suffering from asthma or hay fever. It was soon discovered, though, that the Benzedrine inhaler could be used for other purposes. If the inhaler was opened up, it was found to contain wadding that had been soaked in amphetamine. If the wadding was then put in coffee, a fizzy drink or alcohol the result was a beverage of considerable power. B Bombs, as they became known, were jazzman Charlie Parker's introduction to drugs. They were also the first taste of

NOW, of course, it sounds crazy that amphetamines were once used to treat hyperactive children. In today's more enlightened society, kids may not be prescribed speed, but around five million children in North America are each day given the prescription drug Ritalin.

Debate rages about whether Ritalin, or methylphenidate, is a suitable treatment for children diagnosed with 'attention deficit disorder'. Some experts describe the drug as akin to a 'mild speed'. Others simply call it 'coke for kids'. According to the *American Journal of Psychiatry*, oral consumption of Ritalin produced results comparable to snorting cocaine.

Ritalin now even seems to moving into the world of recreational drug abuse. *Prozac Nation* author Elizabeth Wurtzel is not alone in finding Ritalin tablets lacking in 'the nasal intimacy of cocaine' and so resorting to pulverising them into something snortable. Other enthusiasts are known to be injecting themselves with Ritalin.

uppers for many of the Beat generation writers, including Jack Kerouac, Allen Ginsberg and William S. Burroughs. B Bombs were also discovered by a certain group of 1950s Liverpool students. 'The first drugs I ever took,' recalled John Lennon, 'I was still at art school with the group (we all took it together), was Benzedrine from the inside of an inhaler ...'

As with opium and cocaine in previous generations, amphetamines were marketed in a range of forms. These included not only the Benzedrine inhaler but also pep pills or brain pills. Amphetamines were also recommended for a range of ailments including schizophrenia, travel sickness, hyperactivity and impotence. During the 1930s speed was promoted to help treat depression during the Depression, while a report in 1946 detailed 39 different disorders for which Benzedrine was the recommended treatment.

One area in which amphetamines proved particularly effective was weight loss. During the 1940s in the USA 1,000 amphetamine pills could be legally purchased for 75 cents. Because they speed up the metabolism, there was nothing like them for getting the weight off. One amphetamine-fuelled

ADVERTISING slogans used to promote amphetamine-based products:

'Re-energise for life in the fast lane'

'Come alive'

'Feel good'

'Two pills are better than one month's vacation'

slimmer, Katherine Carson of Texas, was given a prize of $5,000 after successfully losing 57 kilograms (126 pounds) in just four months.

 ## It could never happen today

The discovery of illegal drugs as the active ingredients in apparently harmless general sale products does of course persist to this day. Pharmaceutical companies continue to launch new products, the true nature and effects of which may only become clear after months or years of widespread use and/or abuse. Even established illegal drugs continue to crop up occasionally in mundane products. A German marijuana beer reportedly exists, while some health food stores in the USA recently found themselves in trouble, when they were discovered to be selling cocaine in the form of teabags.

Traditional coca tea, or mate de coca, is still widely available in parts of South America. It is recommended as a remedy for stomach complaints and altitude sickness. Coca is an excellent natural source of vitamins and minerals. It is also, of course, the source of cocaine. Visitors to countries like Peru are these days strongly warned about the problems they will encounter if they attempt to take any mate de coca back to Europe or the USA as gifts for the folks at home. Unfortunately, it seems nobody told this to a certain group of American health food stores. By putting mate de coca on the shelves, they were unwittingly selling teabags containing class A drugs. The authorities, of course, soon put them straight on the matter. Before this, however, at least one customer had tried to take full advantage of the situation. He managed to make himself a little agitated. Then again, he had just drunk a cup of tea brewed from no less than 80 teabags.

THE AUTHORITIES

'Using illegal drugs is against the law.'

– George Bush

 New drug terror

The introduction of new drugs over the past 500 years has almost always provoked suspicion and extreme reactions from the authorities. When tobacco first appeared in Europe, King James I was so alarmed he wrote a 'Treatise on Tobacco' warning against it. In 18th-century Russia, the Czar banned tobacco use outright. Anyone found guilty of this pernicious new drug habit could be punished by being flogged, deported to Siberia or, most charmingly, by having their nose slit open. And those were the punishments for first-time offenders. If a tobacco abuser was convicted on a second offence, the penalty was frequently death. Similarly, in the Ottoman Empire, Sultan Murad IV decreed the death penalty for smoking, and it was noted that 'wherever the

IN the 1700s attempts were made to make coffee an illegal substance in England. In Prussia, Frederick II also tried to ban coffee. Frederick believed that coffee threatened the balance of trade, the profits of his country's breweries and the fitness of his soldiers. A special police force was employed to sniff out illegal coffee roasting establishments.

Sultan went on his travels or on a military expedition his halting-places were always distinguished by a terrible rise in executions. Even on the battlefield he was fond of surprising men in the act of smoking, when he would punish them by beheading, hanging, quartering or crushing their hands and feet.' Even these extreme forms of tobacco health warning, however, did not deter people from carrying on smoking.

In the late 18th century, the Chinese Emperor began to get worried about his country's increasing opium consumption. Striving to be tough on opium and tough on the causes of opium, he announced that anyone found in possession would be executed by means of strangulation. In 1799 he issued a proclamation to prohibit the import, use and cultivation of the drug. Unfortunately, he was up against the greatest and most determined drug dealer of all time – the British Empire.

In the following century, despite direct appeals to Queen Victoria, the trade in opium (produced in British-governed India and exported by one means or another into China) was still going on. Wars were fought over the matter (resulting incidentally in the ceding of Hong Kong to Britain by the Treaty of Nanking), and by the end of the 19th century it is estimated that over 25 per cent of the adult Chinese population were addicted to opium.

 ## Racist scares

As we have seen, in Britain and the USA what we now identify as class A drugs were once freely available for general sale. The change in attitude that led to their criminalisation came about for many reasons. Among them was the fear of ethnic minorities. In the USA, opiate drugs in particular gained their evil reputation because they were associated with the Chinese. Cocaine did likewise because of its association with blacks, and the pattern repeated itself again when Mexican workers were observed enjoying the effects of marijuana.

In the 19th century, thousands of Chinese labourers had been brought into the USA to work on the railways and in the gold mines of the west. Later in the century, however, these areas of industry required much less manpower, so the Chinese had to look elsewhere for employment. The result was that white Americans found themselves in competition for jobs with the Chinese.

Unrest and resentment against the Chinese grew, and began to be expressed in the newspapers published by William Randolph Hearst. Hearst took over the *San Francisco Examiner* in 1887 and began an anti-Chinese campaign based on the myth of 'the Yellow Peril'. Hearst's readers were terrified by images of Chinese fiends stealing American women away to the white slave trade and forcing them into prostitution. It was, of course, obvious how the Chinese seduced white women into such a life. They got them addicted to their own favourite drug – opium. In 1882 Chinese immigration was stopped, and in 1909 the importation of opium for smoking was banned.

Aside from Hearst, another figure who helped to change attitudes towards drugs was Richmond Pearson Hobson. Hobson had been lauded as a hero of the Spanish War of the 1890s. In fact his 1898 attempt to block the Spanish fleet in Santiago had resulted in his own ship sinking, his capture and his spending the rest of the war in a Spanish prison in Cuba. Rather than let news of Hobson's embarrassing failure leak out, the American navy decorated him. As a result he became 'the most kissed man in America' and was elected to Congress in 1906.

As a congressman, Hobson sought some significant moral cause with which his name could be associated, and found it in the proposed prohibition of alcohol. However, his crusade in the cause of temperance came to nothing. Following his departure from Congress, prohibition was introduced in the

IN 1911, a character called Harvey Wiley demanded that the now cocaine-free Coca-Cola should be banned for its side-effect of causing boys to masturbate. During a court case against the Coca-Cola company, Wiley demonstrated another danger of the product. In an experiment that he conducted himself, he showed how Coca-Cola could potentially kill a rabbit. Wiley demonstrated this by filling the unfortunate creature's lungs with the fizzy drink. He did not win the court case.

IN New York's marijuana tea pads a man could get high for a quarter. Most of the marijuana was said to be harvested from supplies growing wild on Staten Island or in New Jersey and other nearby states. There were around 500 tea pads in New York City by the mid-1930s.

1917 Volstead Act and with no help from its original champion. Having had his life's cause stolen, Hobson had to find another. This time he settled on a crusade against heroin.

One thing though that undoubtedly led to the growing use of drugs that so alarmed Mr Hobson was the prohibition of alcohol that he himself had originally championed. If people were unable to forget their troubles one way, they would find another. During the 1920s in America, as alcohol became more difficult to obtain and more expensive, 'tea pads' began to open. Tea pads were similar to the speakeasies where illicit alcohol was sold. Instead of alcohol, though, they sold the cheaper and more readily available marijuana.

The cocaine fiends

The perceived assaults on white women by ethnic groups such as the Chinese were, of course, fantastic stories to help sell newspapers. Even more terrifyingly, in the early 20th century newspapers began to make similar charges against the black population.

In 1914, the *New York Times* detailed how 'Negro cocaine "fiends" are a new southern menace'. Nine men in Mississippi, five in North Carolina and three in Tennessee had, according to the *New York Times*, all 'been killed by crazed cocaine takers'. This cocaine clearly had extraordinary effects. Not only did it cause people to completely lose their minds, it also enabled them to develop incredible superhuman powers. One 'Negro cocaine fiend' was reported as having 'a temporary immunity to shock – a resistance to the "knock-down" effects of fatal wounds. Bullets fired into vital parts, that would stop a sane man in his tracks, fail to check the "fiend" – fail to stop his rush or weaken his attack.'

A 'hitherto inoffensive Negro', in Asheville, North Carolina, was similarly reported as having been shot directly in the heart. Despite this 'the shot did not even stagger the man' while 'a second shot into his arm and chest had as little effect'. As the 1914 pamphlet, 'The Drug Habit Menace in the South' detailed, as a result of cocaine-taking, 'sexual desires are increased and perverted, peaceful Negroes become quarrelsome, and timid Negroes develop a degree of "Dutch courage" that is sometimes almost incredible'.

The reason black people were associated with cocaine was because they had been given it by whites. Black workers on southern plantations were given cocaine by their white employers to make them more industrious and happy. Another plus was that the cocaine meant they could work longer without being fed.

Black people were also enthusiastic customers of travelling medicine shows. In the 19th century these were regular sources of tonics and cola drinks containing cocaine. Following emancipation, as blacks began to be seen as a threat by the white population, the cocaine that had become

'WE first fought the heathens in the name of religion, then Communism, and now in the name of drugs and terrorism. Our excuses for global domination always change.'

– Serj Tankian

associated with them began to be seen as dangerous as well.

In 1911, in the *New York Times*, Dr Hamilton Wright described cocaine as 'the most threatening of the drug habits that has ever appeared in this country'. Wright detailed how its use by southern blacks was often 'a direct incentive to the crime of rape'. Among Wright's other claims to fame was persuading a Vermont congressman called David Foster to sponsor a bill to control opiates, cocaine, cannabis and so forth. This bill failed in 1911 but a revived version of it was taken up at Wright's instigation by another congressman, Francis Burton Harrison.

The US Harrison Narcotic Act of 1914 was the model for all subsequent Western drugs legislation. The Harrison Act brought in stringent controls to prevent opium and coca being imported, produced, sold or handled by anyone who had not been officially registered to do so. Essentially, from this moment on if you were a drugs user you were also, automatically, a criminal.

 ## White slavers in Britain

In Britain, the Empire's involvement with the opium trade resulted in a somewhat different attitude to this drug at least.

The opium trade had, however, gone into decline by the end of the 19th century.

Nevertheless, stories of Chinese opium fiends and white slavers served to titillate the nation's newspaper readers. In November 1918, Billie Carleton, a famous dancing star at the Haymarket Theatre, died as a result of taking drugs. The drug that killed her was, in fact, veronal. She had taken this to get to sleep after taking cocaine earlier the same evening, at a victory party at the Albert Hall to celebrate the end of the war.

Billie Carleton's death resulted in the inquest and trial for manslaughter of a dress designer from the Haymarket Theatre, one Reggie de Veulle. The newspapers weren't slow to build up the whole tale with details of sex orgies and, of course, wicked foreigners. At one party at de Veulle's flat, a Mrs Ada Ping Yu had prepared opium for the gathering. Ada was in fact a Scottish lady but had become a fiendish oriental by virtue of marriage.

Not long after Billie Carleton's case, a less well-known nightclub dancer, Freda Kempton, also died after taking drugs. Again a link was made to Chinese involvement, as her supplier was discovered to be a Regent Street restaurateur with the magnificent name of Brilliant Chang.

In comparison to the US, Britain had fewer black citizens during the post-World War One period. When one was found in the person of Edgar Manning, a black musician and drug dealer, the association between drugs and black people was nevertheless established in the minds of whites.

Undermined by the enemy

Around the time of World War One, it was, of course, another foreign race that particularly concerned the British. Sure enough, the Germans proved to be mixed up in the world of drugs. Heroin had been developed by Bayer, a German company, and cocaine was marketed by Merck, likewise a business venture of the evil Hun.

In February 1916 a sensational court case took place. The accused were Horace Kingsley, an ex-soldier and ex-convict, and Rose Edwards, a prostitute. Kingsley and Edwards's crime was having sold cocaine to Canadian soldiers stationed at Folkestone. In May, an Army Council order forbade the supply of cocaine, opium, codeine, heroin, Indian hemp and morphine to the armed forces except on prescription.

The frontman of the cocaine-selling operation was a former porter at the Café de Paris in London, William Johnson. Under existing law the only charge that could be brought against Johnson, however, was that he had sold a scheduled poison without putting a proper label on it. The case was dismissed.

To tighten up on the legal loopholes that were clearly threatening national security, in July 1916 the Defence of the Realm Act was passed. This made it illegal for anyone except medical men, pharmacists or vets to possess, sell or give away drugs. Thus this act became the first piece of British legislation to deal with substances such as cocaine and opium specifically as 'dangerous drugs'.

Following the death of Billie Carleton, it was recommended that permanent legislation should replace the Defence of the Realm Act. The Dangerous Drugs Act of 1920 therefore, like America's Harrison Act, limited the manufacture, sale, possession and distribution of opiates and cocaine to authorised persons.

Cannabis was not included under the Dangerous Drugs Act for the simple reason that it was not regarded as a dangerous drug. This oversight was soon rectified. A League of Nations conference was held at Geneva in 1925 and produced a convention to regulate drugs distribution. International agreement was given to opiate manufacture being limited to the amounts needed for medical and scientific work. At the request of Egypt, cannabis was also included in this convention because it was 'a dangerous narcotic ... more harmful than opium' and 'about 70 per cent of insane people in lunatic asylums in Egypt are hashiche eaters or smokers'.

As a result of the convention, there was an 82 per cent decline in world opium supplies. Unfortunately, that was just legal opium. The one-time recipients of the British Empire's opium trade, the Chinese, now took the opportunity to move into the illicit opium and heroin production business.

IN the 1920s the Dangerous Drugs Act seemed to get Britain's drug problem finally under control. Prosecutions under the act connected with opium fell from 148 to 36 a year by the end of the decade. Similarly, prosecutions to do with cocaine fell from 65 to 5 a year.

THERE is no evidence of any weight regarding the mental and moral injuries from the moderate use of these drugs… Moderation does not lead to excess in hemp any more than it does in alcohol. Regular, moderate use of ganja or bhang produces the same effects as moderate and regular doses of whisky.

The Report of the Indian Hemp Drug Commission as commissioned by the British government in 1894

How cannabis became a really dangerous drug

In 1930 Harry J. Anslinger was appointed head of the American Federal Bureau of Narcotics. Anslinger's life purpose was to make the United States, and the world in general, fully aware of the drugs menace and to lead the fight against it.

This mission had first been defined when, as a boy of 12, Anslinger was sent into town by the man who lived at the next farm. The neighbouring farmer's wife was a screaming morphine addict and young Harry was dispatched to buy drugs for her. Yes, this story does sound as though it would make more sense if the morphine addict in question was Anslinger's mother, but in relating the tale in his book *The Murderers* Anslinger was adamant that it was a neighbour.

In reality, Anslinger's life mission was perhaps less to do with the fight against drugs than it was with keeping himself in a decent, highly respected job. At first, however, things did not go well. It was, of course, not Anslinger's FBN but rather the FBI, under J. Edgar Hoover, that got all the attention and most of the funding. In fact, soon after the FBN was created the American government drastically cut its budget.

In 1935 Anslinger went into hospital with nervous strain. On his return, he only survived being sacked for ineptitude thanks to the new campaign that he launched. Anslinger made it clear that he was the only person who could save America from a vicious new drugs menace that was poised to sweep the nation – marijuana.

Back in the early 20th century, marijuana was a substance used by immigrant Mexican labourers in the US to relax after a day's toil. It was regarded with suspicion by white Americans and scare stories, similar to those associated with cocaine and the blacks, began to circulate about Mexican marijuana use. In 1914 the El Paso Ordinance was passed prohibiting the possession and sale of cannabis. The Ordinance was, in fact, passed to keep the Mexicans under control following an attack on a group of white Texans by a Mexican gang allegedly driven insane after taking marijuana.

Anslinger wanted each of the individual American states to commit financial resources to the war on drugs that he was heading. In the midst of the Depression, only nine of the then 48 states responded. If the growing unease about marijuana could be worked into a major drugs scare, however, the response might improve.

So Anslinger made marijuana out to be even more terrifying in its effects than opium. He served up horrific stories of crimes committed by individuals out of their minds on the drug. Thanks to these tales, Anslinger's reputation was strengthened not just in America but also on the world stage through League of Nations conferences. The crimes and effects attributed to marijuana nevertheless seem somewhat surreal. In 1937, the *American Magazine* ran the following story:

> *In Los Angeles, California, a youth was walking along a downtown street after inhaling a marijuana cigarette. For many addicts, merely a portion of a 'reefer' is enough to induce intoxication. Suddenly, for no reason, he decided that someone had threatened to kill him and that his life was in danger. Wildly he looked around him. The only person in sight was an aged bootblack. Drug-crazed nerve centres conjured the innocent old shoe-shiner into a destroying monster. Mad with fright, the addict hurried to his room and got a gun. He killed the old man and then later babbled his grief over what had been wanton, uncontrolled murder. 'I thought someone was after me,' he said. 'That's the only reason I did it. I had never seen the old fellow before. Something just told me to kill him!' That's marijuana.*

The most sensational of all the 1930s 'marijuana crimes' occurred in Florida on 16 October 1933, when 21-year-old Victor Licata killed his mother, father, two brothers and a sister with an axe. It was claimed that he committed the murders 'under influence of a marijuana dream'. Licata was

'CANNABIS is a lot less dangerous than rum punch, whisky, tobacco and glue. All of which are legally available.'
    – Paul McCartney, following his 1980 drugs bust in Japan

indeed a known user of marijuana. Perhaps more relevant, though, was the fact that when Victor Licata killed his mother and father he simultaneously killed his aunt and uncle. He was the child of first cousins. One of his siblings had been insane and Victor Licata himself was criminally insane.

By 1937, however, there was a public clamour for action against marijuna. All the American states signed up to Anslinger's Uniform Narcotics Act. The Marijuana Tax Act was signed in the same year, and a 58-year-old Denver man called Samuel R. Caldwell was the first to be convicted and sentenced to hard labour under its provisions.

Any suggestion that the war on drugs should be eased, or that drugs like cannabis were not as dangerous as had been suggested, were quashed by Anslinger. Anyone who disagreed with him found themselves discredited, undermined or even identified as an agent of the drugs industry. A report into 'The Marijuana Problem in the City of New York', commissioned by the mayor of New York from 31 impartial scientists, found that marijuana did not, in fact, lead to violence or tend to change people's personalities. As this was completely the reverse of what he had been telling people, Anslinger had as many copies of the report destroyed as possible.

The gateway drug

Following World War Two there was an all-time low of 20,000 heroin addicts in the USA. Nevertheless, during the 1950s

GREAT official drug research programmes:

Project Chatter Run from 1947 by the US Navy to develop a truth drug following the discovery that Nazi doctors at Dachau had experimented with mescaline.

Project Bluebird Run from 1950 by the CIA to research uses of drugs including ether, morphine and mescaline for use in interrogation.

Operation MK-Ultra Run from 1953 by the CIA to research mind control and drugs during the Cold War. LSD was given to new trainees to test their stamina.

Investigation into the 'common cold' Run by MI5/ MI6 from 1953 at Porton Down in collaboration with the CIA to develop a truth drug. Involved giving volunteer servicemen LSD without their knowledge. *Spycatcher* author and ex-MI5 scientist Peter Wright stated, 'The whole area of chemical research was an active field in the 1950s. I was co-operating with MI6 in a joint programme to investigate how far the hallucinatory drug LSD could be used in interrogations, and extensive trials took place at Porton. I even volunteered as a guinea pig on one occasion.'

CIA Prison Inmate study In 1961 the CIA gave a group of American convicts increasing doses of LSD for 75 consecutive days.

Anslinger kept drugs fear on the boil by introducing a new concept to the debate. Smoking marijuana, Anslinger told the world, led people to go on to heroin use. In the era of the McCarthy communist witch hunts, Anslinger made it clear that behind every narcotics dealer there was a communist plotting to overthrow the government. Indeed, it was generally believed at the time that drugs originated in communist China.

Anslinger often asserted that drug trafficking could be eliminated if users were compulsorily given prison sentences. Thanks to a Louisiana congressman, Hale Boggs, such sentencing was brought into law in 1951. In contravention of evidence that he was known to have seen, Anslinger told the Boggs bill congressional hearings that heroin users 'took to the needle when the thrill of marijuana was gone'. The Narcotic Control Act of 1956 went on to put marijuana on the same level as heroin in the eyes of the law.

The Boggs Act did not deter drug use and end trafficking as Anslinger had confidently predicted. So a lot of people were put into prison. In the state of Missouri in the 1950s, conviction for marijuana possession carried a life sentence. In one year, in the 1970s, under President Nixon's intensified war against marijuana, 226,000 arrests were made. One individual, John Sinclair, was sentenced to 10 years for the possession of two joints. When, in 1973, the state of Oregon took the step of decriminalising marijuana they found no increase in drug use resulted in the next four years. The state had, however, saved a significant amount of money on the law enforcement that had been devoted to the possession and use of marijuana.

UNDER current British law, taking drugs is not strictly illegal. Possessing and supplying drugs are, however, criminal offences, with the latter attracting the harsher penalties. So, if you can find a way to take drugs without possessing them or having them supplied to you, you might just get away with it.

Class A stuff

In Britain throughout the 1950s and 60s, further drugs legislation was introduced, including the Dangerous Drugs Act of 1964, which extended the range of cannabis offences in the UK, and the Drugs (Prevention of Misuse) Act 1964 covering amphetamines. Despite the legislation the number of drug users and addicts increased at an alarming rate. In the 1950s, as far as the Home Office was aware, there were less than 400 British drug addicts.

Today in Britain, amid much controversy, the government has proposed changing the classification of cannabis from a class B to a class C drug. This classification of drugs into A, B and C categories itself derives from the 1971 Misuse of Drugs Act. The 1971 Act remains the central piece of legislation used to control drug use in the UK.

The Dutch experience

The Netherlands is frequently cited as a country that has legalised drugs. In fact, possession of cannabis is still illegal in the Netherlands. The difference in approach from Britain and the USA is that in the Netherlands drugs are seen as a public health and welfare issue. Law enforcement is regarded as being of limited or secondary importance in the Dutch fight against drugs. So in practice although possession of small amounts of cannabis can result in a fine or a month's prison sentence, you shouldn't run into too much trouble if you carry 5 grams or less of cannabis around the streets of Holland.

Home-grown cannabis is also sold in the 1,500 or so cannabis cafés in Amsterdam. These sell on average 0.4 to 2 grams of cannabis to 50 to 300 customers each day. Theoretically, the act of selling the drug is still a crime. Nevertheless, the cafés are tolerated as they provide a place in which to take soft drugs away from the criminal underworld and the harder substances that serious dealers would be keen for their punters to trade up to.

If, however, you want an example of a country that did overcome its drugs problem, you might want to take a look at Harry Anslinger's red menace. China probably had the most complete victory in its war on drugs in the 1940s. It is

IN 1947 one Chinese opium smuggler carried his drugs by dissolving them in water and then soaking the water into a cloth. After drying the now opium-imbued cloth he hopped on a bus to take it to its destination. Unfortunately for him, it was a hot day and the bus had standing room only. Before too long the unmistakable aroma of opium was wafting through the crowd. The hapless smuggler was subsequently executed.

estimated that in 1946 there were 40,000,000 opium smokers in China. When the communists came to power, they virtually eradicated the problem overnight. How on earth did they do it?

TRANSPORT OF DELIGHTS

 Smuggling

Drugs – a rush of excitement through the veins, feelings of paranoia and danger, despair, sickness, death, euphoria and unusual moments of intimacy with complete strangers. Yes, these are the some of the effects not just of taking drugs but of trying to sneak them through customs.

Just to make drugs a little more dangerous than they are already, elaborate systems have evolved for getting the merchandise from its point of origin to its end user. In coun-

 THE international drugs trade is currently believed to be worth around $400 billion each year – accounting for around 8 per cent of all world trade and making the drugs industry the third largest business in the world.

tries all over the globe, incredible amounts of government money are ploughed into stopping this traffic. Smugglers face all manner of barriers – problems with customs, police investigation and imprisonment. Huge hauls of drugs are regularly picked up, and beaming law officials are photographed in front of seizures of illegal imports.

And yet there doesn't seem to be any particular shortage of drugs getting through. The fact that they do so, despite all the many barriers thrown up against them, is surely a testimony to greed, desperation, dogged determination and immense ingenuity.

 ## Sources and trade routes

According to a recent report, it is now easier to move goods – both legal and illegal – around the world than ever before. Whether travelling from South America, Asia or Africa, drugs, a bit like love, always seem to find a way.

Colombian cocaine goes by light aircraft to the Caribbean or by road to the South American coast before the trip to the USA or Europe by sea or air. Peruvian cocaine, on the other hand, tends to move east through Brazil and thence either up to the USA or, alternatively, across the Atlantic to Nigeria and down to South Africa before reaching expectant European nostrils.

Heroin and opium from Afghanistan flow west through Iran or Central Asia and thence into Turkey and eastern Europe. From there they ultimately find their way to users in Britain, Holland or Germany. While the USA's opiates also used to come from Asia, an industry has now developed in South America. The primary suppliers of heroin to the United States are now Colombia, Mexico and, to a lesser extent, Venezuela and Peru.

Drugs don't just enter the USA from the south however. Canada is also being used by drugs traffickers as a route for cannabis, heroin and synthetic drugs such as methamphetamine. In return cannabis and cocaine pass from the US into Canada. Drugs may be transported by sea, across the Great Lakes, along the St Lawrence River or even on foot across the border.

Europe is more self-sufficient as regards synthetic drugs such as ecstasy, amphetamines and LSD. Around 10 to 20 per cent of British requirements of these drugs are produced within the UK, while the Netherlands is described by some commentators as the Colombia of synthetics. These days laboratory-produced synthetic drugs such as ecstasy are being trafficked out of Europe to parts of Africa and the Middle East. At the same time, the market for synthetics such as ecstasy, methamphetamine, paramethoxyamphetamine, LSD and PCP in the United States is growing, leading to a proliferation of 'bucket labs' in North America.

Larger consignments of trafficked drugs may be carried by aircraft and perhaps dropped to be picked up from the ocean by small boats from their destination country. Alternatively, boats carrying merchandise may rendezvous at sea with speed boats ready to carry the cargo ashore. There have even been cases were submarines have been used to transport drugs. Luxury yachts may be used rather

TRANSPORT OF DELIGHTS

IF you don't want to risk carrying drugs across an international border, an alternative might be to go underneath it. In December 2001 American federal authorities discovered a tunnel that had been constructed under the Mexican border. The tunnel began under a house in Nogales, 89 kilometres (55 miles) south of Tucson, and ran for 26 metres (85 feet) to a steel utility plate on the Mexican side of the border. It was estimated that around $21 million worth of cocaine and marijuana had passed through the tunnel into the USA.

more regularly, particularly in areas such as Miami or southern Spain. These prove a particularly effective means to carry drug merchandise as they tend to be less conspicuous and less prone to being raided than smaller or more delapidated vessels.

By road, container lorries offer a multitude of hiding places, but drugs also cross borders in smaller quantities carried by motorists or even bikers. Motorbikes gain a potential smuggling advantage by usually being the first vehicles to disembark from ferries and then passing through customs relatively quickly. Smugglers have also been known to stuff the internal panelling of camper vans with drugs, as officials usually think twice about dismantling vehicles during customs checks. One elderly couple regularly transported drugs stuffed into the seats of their family car beneath their grandchildren. When they were finally arrested and imprisoned, the children were placed in care until their parents could travel out to reclaim them.

Innocent-looking objects

The methods used to sneak drugs in and out of different countries show endless resourcefulness and imagination. The odd objects that have been picked up by customs officials and found to have drugs hidden inside them are legion: flower stems, tyres, wine glasses, hollowed-out roofing tiles, hollowed-out planks, cement posts, lead ingots, electrical transformers, pressurised oxygen cylinders, fruit, bars of soap, coat hangers, dolls, toys, tins of paella. You name it.

In one famous case in 1969, a New Jersey hairdresser was arrested after trying to bring several hundred ski poles into the USA. Each ski pole turned out to be packed with 160 grams of heroin. In 2002, £20 million worth of heroin and cocaine was found on its way into Britain hidden in a consignment of glue containers. As if glue wasn't dangerous enough already.

Heroin has also been transported through the post. Letters have been discovered that have been impregnated with the drug before posting. On receipt, the addressee would soak the letter to release the substance. Postcards have also been

ONE Persian carpet importer was known to transport heroin by sprinkling it over his carpets like some narcotic form of Shake and Vac powder. Once received at the other end of the shipping route, the carpet was given the once-over with a vacuum cleaner and the powder, picked up in the dust bag, was sold for enormous profit.

carefully split into two halves, filled with heroin and then stuck back together to be sent through the mail.

During the Vietnam war in the 1970s, heroin was smuggled back to the US inside the body bags used to carry fallen soldiers home for burial. Some of the corpses were found to have drugs concealed deep within wounds on their bodies.

In June 2000, police at Bogata Airport intercepted a consignment of 215 fake Bon-Bon-Bum brand children's lollipops. These turned out to contain not the bubble gum centre that they were supposed to have, but 21 grams of cocaine each. The street value of the lollipops was estimated at around $7,000 each. Surely beyond the pockets of most small children.

Masters of disguise

Rather than hiding your drugs inside something, you could always just disguise them. Opium has been formed into peanut-like shapes. Then, to make them look really realistic, the opium nuts were inserted into ground nut shells. A similar trick was used in 1952 to get opium from Afghanistan and Pakistan into India. The opium was put into empty walnut shells, and the shells were resealed and mixed with a consignment of ordinary walnuts. The smugglers then made one fatal error. They didn't send their nuts by bulk consignment as you would normally transport walnuts. Instead, they sent their product by parcel post. Customs authorities were quick to realise that these must be very special walnuts indeed.

Morphine has been transported mixed with flour or rice.

IN 1997 in Ashdod, Israel, a 93-year-old woman was arrested for trying to sell heroin to two police officers who had knocked on her door. It was believed that as the woman's eyesight was failing she had mistaken the officers for two of her regular customers.

Colombian cocaine was regularly shaped and coloured to look like Colombia's other principal export, coffee beans. In fact this scam was so prevalent that it was estimated at one point that 5 per cent of all the coffee coming out of Colombia was, in fact, cocaine.

Cocaine has also been solidified and shaped into objects such as ashtrays and even furniture. In one case, cocaine was fashioned into a consignment of fibreglass pet carriers. A consignment of these carriers turned up in Miami from that well-known pet product manufacturing centre, Colombia. They were seized by American Special Agents who cut and ground them up in a heavy-duty meat grinder (it should be mentioned that there were no pets inside them at the time). The ground-up material was then treated with a solvent and the resulting extract dried in a microwave. Yes, it was cocaine. Five kilograms (11 pounds) mixed into the fibreglass of each separate pet carrier.

Above suspicion

On the other hand, you could just be a bit more brash about the whole business. Why not try and smuggle drugs into the USA using, say, the official flagship of your country's naval service? And in just which country might people do such a thing as this? In 1976 the Colombian Navy flagship, *The Gloria*, was invited to take part in the American bicentennial celebrations. On its first stop in Miami, two members of the crew were detained, along with 6 kilograms (13 pounds) of cocaine that had been hidden in the ventilation system. *The Gloria* continued her voyage up the eastern US seaboard before eventually sailing proudly up the Hudson River. At every stop the ship made on its route, more cocaine was apprehended.

Diplomatic ambassadors are obviously highly respected individuals who have worked their way up to positions of supreme responsibility. Appointed as foreign representatives by their governments, they are clearly people of the highest moral standards and are therefore allowed to pass through international customs on diplomatic passports without being searched or having their belongings checked. What a fantastic opportunity to smuggle drugs.

In 1971, the Laotian diplomat Prince Sopsaisana was apprehended by customs officials at Orly Airport in Paris. It was, of course, the most terrible insult to any foreign government to suggest that their chosen representative might be carrying drugs. Prince Sopsaisana was discovered to have 60 kilograms (132 pounds) of pure heroin in his suitcase. As he had diplomatic immunity, he was not put on trial in France but was instead asked to leave the country. Back home in Laos, Prince Sopsaisana conspicuously still didn't have any charges brought against him.

Stuffing and swallowing

Of course the most popular container for smuggling drugs is the human body itself. The human body has been an inspiration to artists through the ages. For drug traffickers it is a useful mobile device, full of flaps, folds, lumps, bumps and dark hidden places, all surely put there for the specific purpose of smuggling drugs. Yes, we're in the world of stuffers and swallowers.

One of the most popular methods of smuggling drugs is to stuff the material under your clothes or inside your body. A member of Colombia's internationally renowned horse-breeding and cocaine-trafficking Ochoa family was once apprehended travelling with 1.5 kilograms (3¼ pounds) of powder stuffed in her bra.

There are other variations on the smuggling drugs in and about your person method. A one-legged smuggler was found with drugs hidden inside his hollowed-out wooden leg. Another smuggler, picked up in the early 1990s, had obviously decided he didn't want the continued unpleasantness associated with hiding drugs inside his body by the usual methods of swallowing or stuffing. So, he had had a bit of cosmetic surgery done. When he was picked up by the authorities, drugs were found in his buttocks. Literally in his buttocks. He had had pockets carved into each cheek of his behind.

Another tale of hacking special storage compartments into the bodies of unfortunate individuals involved a none too bright South American boxer. Recruited by a drugs gang to smuggle cocaine into the USA, he had a simple minor operation to help secrete the illegal substances. Unfortunately, the operation was not done with his full consent. The gang sliced his thigh open, packed the drugs inside and then clumsily stitched him up. On the plane to the US, the brusque nature of the surgery resulted in blood poisoning. The boxer collapsed before he could make his delivery and was picked up by the authorities. Despite treatment he lost a leg. This turned out to have been a relatively lucky development. When the drugs gang were arrested, it was found that their intention had been to kill the boxer as soon as the drugs reached their destination.

To stuff drugs up your lower orifices you need a 'charger'. A charger is a metal or sturdy rubber container. You fill this with your drugs, seal it carefully and then, if you want to make life a little easier for yourself, spread a bit of Vaseline over it. The charger is then pushed up inside your body into the secret luggage container of your choice: front or back if you're a lady, probably just the back option if you're a gent. Once you've done that, you can waddle off to check in at the airport.

If you don't fancy being a stuffer, then it's swallowing for you.

To prepare drugs for swallowing, pack them into condoms or some other form of soft rubber. The condom prepared for swallowing should be filled with just a few grams of drugs until it is about the size of a large grape. Indeed, to get used to the procedure, drugs carriers, or mules, practise by swallowing whole grapes without chewing. Presumably, though, somewhere in the world somebody has made the mistake of packing their condom as large as it will go before proceeding to choke themselves trying to swallow the large, densely packed balloon.

The condom then has to be tied up. Dental floss is often favoured for this. Unlike cotton thread, it stretches and is also less likely to dissolve when bombarded with acids while the package is lying in your stomach. Once the pack is tied up, you might again like to make life a little easier for yourself by smearing it with syrup to help it slide down your throat. Don't forget, though, you don't just have to swallow one.

A bit like Olympic athletes, swallowers have been consistently improving their performance through the decades. A few years ago, 30 or so containers in one person was considered good going. The average more recently was up to 70 to 80. In October 1995, a Mr Basudev Parajuli, a 26-year-old from Katmandu, was found to have swallowed at least 103 packs, containing a total of 1 kilogram (2¹/₂ pounds) of heroin, valued at $460,000. Think he's the world record holder? British customs officers once picked up an individual who had ingested 260 packs. How on earth do they do it? They must be on drugs.

Once you've stuffed or swallowed your consignment and got on your aeroplane, the problems really start. During your journey it is, of course, imperative that you avoid having to pass a motion. If you do have to pop to the loo mid-flight, presumably you have to give the packs a bit of a rinse in the hand basin before glugging them back down again. When you arrive at your destination and successfully pass through customs, your merchandise can finally be allowed to pass through you.

Obviously this method is extraordinarily dangerous. If any one of the condoms inside you splits, the large quantity of drugs released will probably be sufficient to kill you. And if things even start to go wrong in this way, the people you're carrying the substance for may want to get the rest of their expensive consignment back in a hurry. Swallowing drugs in order to carry them essentially turns you into a large walking package. If the owners of the product decide they want to get their merchandise back, they may well do what people normally do when they want to open a package in a hurry. There are, indeed, plenty of instances of the remains of drugs mules being found dumped in the middle of nowhere, hacked open in an attempt to retrieve the usable drugs inside them.

If you manage to avoid being hacked open, you may still be forced to undergo an intimate body search by a suspicious customs officer. If you are picked out for such treatment it will probably mean being kept in a room for 24 hours or more while the customs officers sit and wait until you defecate. Obviously, the nature of the operation means that when the need for this function arises, you don't get to go away into a private toilet cubicle. Some airports will, for example, provide you with a transparent toilet on a podium.

You may be put in leg irons while you are held or even have to undergo a rectal and/or vaginal search and/or have your stomach pumped. The success rate in apprehending drug smugglers this way is estimated at around 15 per cent of those detained. So 85 per cent of those who are detained, held for hours, forced to defecate in front of customs officers

and subjected to internal body searches are completely innocent. The reason why so many blameless individuals are
picked out for such treatment might well be questioned.
Customs agents in Chicago obviously regarded the whole
procedure as a bit of a perk of their job. They were discovered to have detained and searched significantly more
women than men.

Drugs mule is probably not anyone's choice of a fulfilling
career. One such Colombian smuggler, Porota, was interviewed by the BBC when she was five years into a prison
sentence for drugs smuggling:

*I am very nervous at the moment because I have been
granted parole later this month, and I don't want
anything to go wrong. I need to get out of prison
because I have three children: one aged 12, one aged
11 and one aged 10 ... I carried drugs because I had no
help supporting my children and things were very difficult for us. You will do whatever you have to do for your
children. I wanted them to have a better life, without so
much hardship ... The most difficult thing is not being
with my children. They never said to me, 'Mummy we
want you to buy us a little house.' It was what I wanted
for them. That's why I did it. For a house. My mother
had died and we were left with no house ... My children
think that I'm working here in England. I have had very
little communication with them. They live in the country-
side, with an uncle of mine who is very strict. I have only
been allowed to speak to them three times in these four*

IN 1972 President Nixon launched Operation Intercept, deploying 2,000 US customs agents to check all vehicles crossing the border from Mexico. After three weeks, with practically no finds of drugs and no dent in the general drug traffic, the operation was abandoned.

years. Would I ever carry drugs again? No, no, no. No. Never. If I could turn the clock back, I would not do it. I feel very guilty that my children are sad and maybe feel abandoned by their mother. When I return to Colombia I will tell them the truth.

At a guess, Porota was probably not a particularly significant figure in the international drugs business. But then the more significant figures don't usually get caught carrying drugs through customs themselves.

 ## Stuffed animals

While actual mules aren't often used for trafficking drugs, plenty of other animals have been. In 1993, a consignment of 300 boa constrictors was picked up by US authorities. All of the snakes had had cocaine-packed condoms stuffed inside them. Not only that but the smugglers had come up with a radically different way of keeping the snakes' bowels in check while in transit. Each one of the boas had had its rectum sewn up to keep the drugs inside. What kind of people spend their time sewing up the backsides of several hundred unfortunate reptiles?

A few years later, someone else tried the same trick. Obviously by this time the smugglers thought the authorities would be wise to large groups of boa constrictors. So instead they used iguanas. Once again, the creatures had all had their bottoms sewn up.

Another creature to fall foul of the way drug traffickers treat their pets was an Old English sheepdog spotted one day at JFK Airport looking underweight and ill having arrived from, where else?, Colombia. When X-rayed, the hound's insides turned out to be stuffed with no less then 10 balloon-like condoms, all filled with cocaine. A total weight of 2.5 kilograms (5 pounds) of drugs had been forced into the dog. Examination showed that they had been inside the animal for between two and four weeks, during which, for perhaps obvious reasons, he had not eaten at all. By the time he was picked up, infection had set in, as the condoms had not been sterilised before insertion.

'Coke', as he was subsequently named, was incredibly lucky to survive the ordeal. Subsequently he made a miraculous recovery and is now working for the US Customs service. John Erik Roa, from Paterson, New Jersey, was arrested

OPIUM was once smuggled into the USA inside the horns of a herd of cattle. Each cow's horns had been hacked off, hollowed out, packed with opium and then, with the addition of a screw thread, reattached to the animal. And they would have got away with it too, if an eagle-eyed customs officer hadn't spotted one of the animals coming through with a horn hanging off at an unusual angle.

AN 84-year-old Michigan woman, Lillian Howard, was arrested for attempting to smuggle marijuana to her son in her underwear during a prison visit.

when he arrived to pick up coke (that's both the substance and the dog).

A female Chinese smuggler was picked up with her cat and its litter of kittens. The cat was OK. Although probably not feeling too cheerful. The kittens were conspicuous by their lack of movement. Each of them had been drowned, dried out, hollowed out, stuffed with drugs and then put back in the basket with mum. These drug smugglers are clearly no friends to innocent animals.

Is there then nothing drug traffickers won't stoop to? No, there isn't. Pablo Escobar's right-hand man, Carlos Lehder, tried to smuggle drugs into the US using his own mother as a carrier. On the plus side, there are no reports that he had to sew her bottom up for the journey.

The dead baby

Using your own mother as a drugs mule may seem extreme, but then there is also the tale of the dead baby.

There are, of course, regular cases of live children being used to smuggle drugs. For example, in February 2002 police arrested two women in eastern Colombia who allegedly headed an operation smuggling cocaine taped to the bodies of small children. However, the dead baby story is of rather more dubious authenticity. 'Let's get this straight right here and now: there is no cocaine-stuffed dead baby, at least at this writing,' proclaims one earnest US internet site, which goes on to berate the way this apparent urban myth has taken hold:

> *The dead baby resurfaces frequently, reported as fact in otherwise responsible and prestigious, and some not so responsible and prestigious, publications. It has appeared on the front page of the* Washington Post, *in* Life Magazine *and in the* National Enquirer. *The story, with minor variations, is that an alert customs official or airlines employee on a Colombia–Miami flight noticed that a baby in the arms of a woman passenger did not look well. Closer scrutiny revealed that it was dead and its body stuffed with high-grade cocaine in an attempt to smuggle the drug into this country.*

Another site, decorated with ominous demonic symbols, tells how all this genuinely happened to the sister of a co-worker of the writer's sister (oh yes, this doesn't sound like an urban myth for a moment). The individual concerned made a trip from Texas into Mexico with her two-year-old child. The child disappeared and within 45 minutes had been murdered. When the child's body was found, it had been hollowed out and filled with drugs so it could be carried back across the border looking as though it was sleeping.

The dead baby story doesn't seem to go away. Another chilling variation on the theme circulated as a news report in

May 2000 in Dubai. In this instance, according to a police-man from the United Arab Emirates, drug smugglers were found to have stuffed their stash into the corpse of a young girl whom they had apparently killed, in a foiled attempt to bring narcotics into the Arab Gulf region. The *Gulf News* quoted Abdul Rahman Naser al-Fardan, head of the police drug squad in Sharjah (one of the seven emirates in the United Arab Emirates) as saying that a woman carrying the dead girl was arrested on arrival at an unnamed Gulf state. An airport official became suspicious when he tried to play with the apparently sleeping child.

Yet another urban myth? The disturbing detail in this version of the tale is the fact that the murdered girl's corpse was not packed with cocaine or heroin or amphetamines or even cannabis. It was stuffed with codeine. Codeine is, like heroin, a derivative of opium and a potentially addictive painkiller. Nevertheless, it is seen in the West as being rela-tively harmless and has been used in a range of headache preparations. Codeine is not freely available in the Gulf states. But would anyone go to the trouble of murdering a child and stuffing the corpse in order to transport headache pills? There again, heroin was originally sold as a cough cure.

TAKE THAT!

 ## Get in there

The journeys across continents that narcotic, hallucinogenic and stimulant substances take is, in many ways, nothing compared to their ultimate journey – from the outside to the inside of the human body. Some substances may have been inside people's bodies while in transit of course, but this time there are no rubber or metal cylinders involved. 'Every conceivable route has been used for getting cannabis into the body,' says Andrew Tyler in *Street Drugs*, making a point that applies, pretty much, to drugs in general.

 ## Giving the needle

Putting stuff in your mouth, chewing and then swallowing is a well-established method of getting it inside your body. Unfortunately, with heroin – unless you're taking it just for the taste – this method simply doesn't work. This is because your body will try to sort the heroin out for you. First your stomach will change it into morphine. The morphine will then come up against your liver, which is fairly efficient at breaking morphine down. So by the time the heroin gets into your bloodstream, it will have lost much of its potency. If, however, you're so minded, you might just bypass your body's natural defence system and jam the drugs straight into your veins.

Injection is the fastest, most direct and most efficient method of getting many drugs inside the body, and in the past century and a half, the hypodermic syringe has become synonomous with illegal drug-taking. Preparing heroin for injection is referred to as cooking up, although you may think this homely image is a sad reflection of the reality.

Heroin is mixed up in water, perhaps with a dash of lemon juice or vitamin C. That's not for taste or even for a bit of a vitamin supplement; it's to help dissolve the mixture. There is then an actual bit of cooking or heating up. This is usually done with a cigarette lighter. The cooker itself is usually a spoon, although the singer Billie Holiday used to use an old tuna fish can to cook up enough to satisfy her prodigious appetite. The cooked-up substances are then drawn into a syringe and injected while warm into the fatty tissue under the skin for skin popping, or straight into a vein for mainlining.

Injection is clearly a dramatic ritual involving not a little bit of performance. In the 1960s, Gerard Malanga, the dancer who appeared in early shows with the Velvet Underground, incorporated a feigned act of shooting up as part of his routine. In the 1970s, the New York Dolls also acted out the ritual on stage. Backstage in the dressing room they were doing the same thing for real.

One stage injection, however, dated back to a more genteel era. In the early years of the 20th century, a stage play about the detective Sherlock Holmes toured theatres. Audiences watched transfixed as, in one scene, William Gillette, the actor playing Holmes, physically injected himself live on stage, presumably with some form of saline solution.

Before the creation of heroin, many people injected themselves with morphine. This drug really took off around 1855, as it was at this time that the hypodermic syringe, as we know it today, was first introduced. The hypodermic was perfected by an Edinburgh doctor called Alexander Wood. Dr Wood had come up with a syringe with a hollow metal needle based, he said, on a bee sting. He arranged for Ferguson, a London instrument maker, to make the device up for him and first used the syringe to inject morphine into a patient in 1853.

One of Wood's claims for his syringe was that it would cure addiction. His belief was that taking drugs by eating them caused people to develop an appetite or a hunger for them, as they would have for any food or drink. Injecting

THE first person to become addicted to morphine injections and the first person to die of a hypodermic-induced overdose are said to be one and the same person: Rebecca Massy, the wife of the syringe's inventor, Alexander Wood. It's a neat but untrue story. Rebecca survived her husband, not dying until 1894.

drugs straight into the bloodstream would surely bypass this problem completely.

Just how wrong this idea was became clear in a few short years after the syringe was introduced. The American Civil War was the first period in which Wood's syringe was widely used, and by the end of it 400,000 American soldiers had become addicted to injecting drugs.

Wood's idea wasn't altogether new. Sir Christopher Wren, the architect of St Paul's Cathedral, had tried injecting dogs using a hollow quill attached to a bulb in 1656 and had gone on to try something similar on humans. In 1664, the English diarist Samuel Pepys had gone to see 'an experiment of killing a dog by letting opium into his hind leg'.

Presumably, though, this wasn't a great success with human beings or dogs, and it wasn't until the 1830s that the technique started to be developed again. A Dr Lafargue used the tip of a lancet dipped in morphine solution and left inserted under the skin to get morphine into the bloodstream. An Irish doctor, Francis Rynd, used a gravity-fed bottle attached to a hollow needle in 1844.

An earlier, more primitive idea which works on similar principles, is detailed in Robert Burton's 17th-century work, *The Anatomy of Melancholy*. As one of his many cures for melancholy, Burton recommends getting hold of a few leeches, the bloodsucking worms so popular with medical practitioners in bygone centuries, and popping them behind your ears for a few minutes. Then, once the leeches have sucked your skin open, Burton says you should rub opium into the resulting sores. This surely is the 17th-century version of skin popping.

Injecting is a possibility for just about everything. Alcohol or even caffeine can be injected if so desired. In fact caffeine, the drug so many of us take every single day in coffee, tea and soft drinks, can be devastating if taken in its pure crystallised form. Some pushers have been known successfully to pass off humble caffeine as amphetamines or even cocaine.

Although it's normally taken as 'white snuff', cocaine can be injected, as it is soluble. It only gives a short hit (a few minutes), so users opting for this method can find themselves injecting up to 15 times a day. People have also been known to inject crack cocaine which isn't soluble. They get around this by mixing it with vitamin C or heating it with water or alcohol. The resulting substance is relatively lumpy and sticky, so it's still not possible to get it through a normal hypodermic needle. Those determined to go for this option therefore have to get hold of larger bore veterinary needles.

 ## Taking opium

Arguably, the modern notion of drug abuse began with the writer Thomas De Quincey, who was among the first Europeans to take drugs for pleasure rather than as a medical treatment. De Quincey took opium dissolved in wine in the form of laudanum. The title he gave his best known work, *The Confessions of an English Opium Eater*, is therefore inaccurate.

Opium had been eaten for over 1,500 years in India, but generally this was not a popular method of consumption. Raw opium is a bitter substance likely to make you throw up violently on at least the first few occasions you take it. So Europeans like De Quincey took it with its taste disguised as laudanum, while Turks ate it with spices such as nutmeg, cardamom, cinnamon or mace.

In China, the East Indies and what are now Vietnam and Taiwan, a new method of taking opium gained popularity. Using a pipe to smoke opium, in what became known as an opium den, became one of the most notorious methods of drug-taking in the late 19th and early 20th centuries.

It is now argued that the notion of the opium den was something of a myth. There were few, if any, establishments that existed solely for the purposes of opium-taking. Places that were described as opium dens were usually just some sort of social club with opium-smoking – one of the many ways in which Chinese seamen spent their leisure time. In the late 19th century, a reporter sent by the *Morning Advertiser* newspaper to expose the full horror of the opium dens didn't find the sordid spectacle he expected. 'It was not repulsive,' he had to admit. 'It was calm. It was peaceful.'

Mrs Frank Leslie recorded what she saw when she visited another such 'opium den' in San Francisco in 1877. Coming off a 'perfectly dark' courtyard, she entered 'a small, close, but apparently clean room' in which could be detected the fumes of burning opium, these being 'not disagreeable' and reminiscent of roasting groundnuts. Finding herself in a room surrounded by double tiers of shelves, Mrs Leslie was not slow to notice that these shelves were almost entirely filled with 'Chinamen'. In fact, some of the shelves held two 'Chinamen' huddled together with a tray between them 'holding a lamp and a horn box filled with the black, semi-liquid paste'.

An opium pipe might be about 50 centimetres (19½ inches) long and 5 centimetres (2 inches) in diameter, and was made mainly of bamboo with a small cup or bowl fixed on the side. In the late 19th century Farmer and Rogers of Regent Street advertised a full opium kit, including pipe, lamps, vessel for oil, boxes and so forth, for sale for ten shillings and sixpence.

The smoker would lie on his side with his pipe in one hand and would take up a pill or lump of opium paste on the end of a metal wire or needle. Next the opium was held to the flame of the lamp and twisted until it became sticky. It was then worked into the bowl of the pipe while the smoker inhaled strongly.

Opium is quick to vaporise, so it was necessary for the smoker to draw all the smoke into his lungs as fast as possible. Ideally this was all done in one go. The smoke was then held in the lungs as long as could be managed. If the opium didn't get into the bloodstream through the lungs, there was a chance it might get in through the nasal membranes, so the smoke was finally blown out through the nostrils.

One pipe lasted between 15 and 30 seconds. It would whistle and gurgle while the smoker worked the opium into the bowl with his needle, according to Mrs Leslie, as 'the spirits of ten thousand previous pipe-loads stirred to life'.

Mrs Leslie described her smoker heating up another pill of opium for another pipe and then another, and another, as long as 'he can control his muscles, until, at last, the nerveless hand falls beside him, the pipe drops from his fingers, and the head falls back in heavy stupor, the face ghastly white, the eyes glazed and lifeless, the breathing stenorous, the mind wandering away in visions like those De Quincey has given to the world in *The Confessions of an English Opium Eater*'.

The smoker would then be unconscious for perhaps 15 minutes for a single pipe, or several hours if he'd smoked a series of them. It is for this reason that smokers lay down to smoke their opium. As with heroin today, the novice opium user would, more often than not, be nauseated by the first pipe and would take several goes to get used to it.

ANCIENT opium pipes can now be valuable collectors' items, but old pipes were already valuable during the days of the opium dens. Unvaporised opium would solidify inside the pipes and could eventually be chipped out and recycled. This already used opium was referred to as 'dross' and was made into pills to be sold to the poor, or mixed with tobacco or tea as a mixture for smoking.

The introduction of smoking

The act of smoking itself was unknown in Europe before 1492 and the introduction of tobacco by Columbus. When a member of Columbus's crew was seen smoking in public, it was declared by the Spanish Inquisition that he must have been possessed by the devil, and he was thrown into prison. Smoking has always been bad for you.

A few years later, in 1535, when the French navigator Jacques Cartier arrived in Canada, he too encountered native people smoking and described them filling 'their bodies with smoke until it comes out of their mouth and nostrils as from a chimney'. He said, 'We tried to imitate them, but the smoke burnt our mouths as if it had been pepper.' Later, in the 16th century, tobacco was popularised in England by Sir Walter Raleigh, and in France by Jean Nicot', after whom the tobacco plant Nicotiana and ultimately the active substance nicotine were named.

 Cannabis-smoking

Cannabis is frequently smoked in a joint, or spliff, with heat-softened resin, or grass, mixed with tobacco. Alternatively, pellets can be heated and their vapours sucked up through a ballpoint pen tube. It can also be heated on a piece of foil or between two knives, and the smoke can be trapped in a milk bottle and sucked up in one go.

Another method of smoking the evil weed is by means of a pipe such as a clay chillum, a brass grill top or a hookah.

'THEY say marijuana leads to other drugs. No, it leads to carpentry. "Hey! This box could be a bong. This ashtray could be a bong ... This guy's head could be an excellent bong."
– Denis Leary

The hookah pipe, like so many concepts in the world of drugs, goes by many names, including narghile, shisha or, less exotically, the hubbly bubbly or bong. The hookah pipe is believed to have originated in Turkey hundreds of years ago and can of course be used for any smokable substance, legal or illegal. It continues to provide a standard method of smoking in the Middle East, being used publicly in restaurants and cafés throughout the region.

Aficionados claim that hookah smoke is much smoother and sweeter than that provided by other smoking methods. Smoke from the hookah is cooled, softened and detoxified by being passed through water. Hookah experts sometimes cool their smoke further still by adding ice cubes to the pipe's water bowl, while others flavour their fumes by adding fruit juice, wine or milk to the bowl. Today the internet abounds with instructions for home-made hookahs, including the standard water bong, the gravity bong, the chamber bong and even the waterfall bong.

During the 1970s, variations on such devices were marketed, such as the dashboard pipe, which could be fixed on the dashboard of your car so you could share a smoke with your date or your driving examiner. A bong frisbee was also marketed so you could toss a smoke to a friend. The *Star Wars* space gun bong, on the other hand, could be used

FEEL THE STRAIN

Although cannabis is a naturally occurring plant, hundreds of varieties now exist not least because of human intervention to develop new, exotic and ever more powerful breeds.

The internet site www.cannabis-strainbase.com is an authoritative and encyclopedic listing and review of an astounding range of varieties, including famous African strains such as African Queen, Ethiopian Highland, Malawi Gold, Swazi Skunk, Tanzanian Magic and Zambian Copper; Asian strains including Himalayan Gold, Kerala Skunk, Mangolian Indica and Nepalese; and New World strains from AweSomeTangerine through Killin Garberville, Lambsbreath, Matanuska Thunder and Schnazzleberry to Williams Wonder and Yumbolt.

The list of European varieties is no less prodigious, including AK-47, Amsterdam Flame, Black Widow, Blue Russian, Chocolate Chunk, Dutch Dragon, Easy Rider, El Nino, Exodus, Hollands Hope, Killer Queen, New York City Diesel, Nirvana Special, Northern Bright, Power Bud, Spontanica, Stonehedge, Twister, Venus, Warlock, White Mr Nice and Wonder Woman.

The strainbase also includes listings for Australian, New World and Hawaiian varieties as well as New Hybrids such as Afghan Delight, Bubbleberry x AK-47, California Sunrise, Cream Sodica, Dream Weaver, Dutch Royal Orange, Mr Bubble, Reclining Buddha, Skunk Kush, Skywalker, Super Titanium Alloy Haze, Swazi Safari, TNT, Ultra Skunk and White Willow.

to blast cannabis smoke into your lungs. It should be pointed out that this last example was probably not official *Star Wars* merchandise.

 ## Cannabis recipes

Of course, for many cannabis is a popular and versatile cooking ingredient. It can be made into tea and drunk, although, apparently, you should let the pot (pardon the pun) stand for a little while longer than for normal tea – about an hour and a half is advised. Recipe books also abound for incorporating cannabis into sweets or cakes, such as hashish fudge, Scooby snacks, cookies, bud bars or canabutter, which can be used, for example, in your brownies or just spread on a piece of toast first thing in the morning.

One advantage of smoking is that, because the effects are felt almost immediately, as soon as you feel you've had enough you can stop. If, though, you've just gobbled up a plate of canabutter-rich brownies, the effects won't hit you so soon. So, by the time you realise you've had too much, it will be too late to do anything about it.

Another aspect of cannabis cookery it's maybe best to avoid is handing in the results to your teacher with your school homework. One slightly over-enthusiastic 13-year-old girl nevertheless did exactly this. In February 2002, a project on the medical benefits of marijuana entitled 'Mary Jane for Pain' was handed in at Mission Hills Junior High School in Santa Cruz, California, complete with a lovingly baked hash muffin by way of practical coursework.

Cocaine-snorting

Cocaine is familiar to many in the affluent West as a white powder. It is chopped finely with a razor blade or credit card on a mirror or similarly hard surface, divided into lines and snorted, perhaps through a straw, perhaps through a specially made jewelled and gold implement or perhaps through a rolled banknote.

The banknote option is clearly a popular one. In 1987, the American Drug Enforcement Agency detected that one-third of the notes at the Federal Reserve Building in Chicago were tainted with cocaine. In October 1999, it was announced that more than 99 per cent of British banknotes showed traces of cocaine. Five per cent of notes in the British study were found to have heightened levels of cocaine. In other words, these had actually been used to snort cocaine. The other notes had been contaminated by being rubbed against the 5 per cent in wallets, cash machines and so on. The amounts of cocaine on the surface of the notes were, however, too minuscule to have an intoxicating effect on even the most sensitive nose.

 Chew on that!

If you are a near penniless peasant living up a mountain some-where in South America you would probably use a different method to take cocaine. It would be ingested by chewing leaves from the coca plant. This has clearly been going on for some time. In the 15th century, Amerigo Vespucci, the man after whom the entire continent was subsequently named, observed what he thought was tobacco-chewing on 'an offshore island along the coast of northern South America'. What he described sounds much more like coca-chewing:

Each had his cheeks bulging with a certain green herb which they chewed like cattle, so that they could scarcely speak. And hanging from his neck each carried two dried gourds one of which was full of the very herb he kept in his mouth; the other full of a certain white flour like powdered chalk. Frequently each put a certain small stick (which had been moistened and chewed in his mouth) into the gourd filled with flour. Each then drew it forth and put it in both sides of his cheeks, thus mixing the flour with the herb which their mouths contained. This they did frequently a little at a time.

The gourd with the green herb, presumably coca leaves, is called a chuspa. The white flour is an alkaline powder such as lime or ash, and the gourd it is carried in is an iscupuru. The alkali could be caustic, so it is important that only a tiny bit is picked up on the end of the small stick and that it is poked into the centre of the wad of leaves in your cheek. The alkali can then be safely diluted by saliva and the pH balance inside the mouth will rise, thereby enabling the cocaine to be better absorbed from the leaves. The wad of leaves is then sucked and kept moving in the mouth rather than actually chewed. The native South Americans even had a word – *cocada* –

which referred to a period of time of around 40 minutes. This unit of time was in fact the period a man could walk for before a pellet was exhausted. One thing Vespucci missed was that the whole business turns your saliva bright green.

 ## Entrances down below

So you can get drugs inside you through your mouth, through your lungs and through your veins. And there is yet a further way by which intoxicating substances can gain entrance to the human body.

A few years ago an American rock group called Lustre King released an unusually titled track. It was, they said, inspired by a magazine article concerning an extremely well-known American female recording star. According to Lustre King, the singer had been told by her doctor that after years of drug abuse, any further cocaine taken nasally would go straight to her brain and she would die. So, with her schnoz no longer an option, the said recording star found an alternative avenue for getting coke inside her body. And thus she became the inspiration for Lustre King's classic track 'Xmas in my Pussy'.

Entrance through the basement is, however, not a wholly mythical way of taking drugs. The reason it works is because drugs like cocaine can be absorbed not only through the mucous membranes in the nose but also through the mucous membrances in the rectum or vagina.

Death might, on the other hand, seem preferable to some of the side-effects of taking drugs through the lower regions.

COCAINE has been believed to have aphrodisiac properties for decades and is frequently linked with stimulated sexual behaviour; addicts often rate cocaine as the most effective drug for increasing libido and sexual responsiveness. Traces of cocaine have been found in semen samples taken shortly after the drug has been used. Tests have shown that cocaine passed in this method does not get the user's sexual partner high, but it may have a grave effect on any resulting child.

In 1988, American doctors warned against a new method of taking cocaine during sex after one 34-year-old American tried injecting cocaine into the shaft of his penis prior to inter-course. Although the said penis remained erect for some time, the experience was, presumably, not the mind-blowing erotic success that had been hoped for. After an erection lasting three whole days, the penis finally subsided, only to cause blood to leak into the tissues of the man's feet, hands, genitals, back and chest. He was taken to hospital, where doctors worked to stop the spread of gangrene. They achieved this by amputating all but one of the man's fingers as well as his legs. The penis fell off of its own accord.

DRUGS TOUR

 The lesser evil

The production of drugs and their raw materials is concentrated in certain areas of the globe. The reasons for this frequently seem to come down to one: despite Uncle Sam's enduring war against drugs, America has often inadvertently assisted in the establishment of local drug industries.

 The Golden Crescent

Opium is now associated with two main areas of production: the Golden Triangle, comprising Burma (or, as its rulers now call it, Myanmar), Laos and Thailand; and the Golden Crescent of Afghanistan, Iran and Pakistan.

Although heroin production was only introduced into Afghanistan during the 1980s, it had been growing opium poppies for many years, and by the time of the 2001

September 11th attacks was said to be supplying 80 per cent of the world's opium. Production had boomed thanks to one thing which has consistently helped the drugs industry: war.

During the 1970s, not only was there war in Afghanistan but it was war against the Soviet Union. The USA was keen to aid such anti-Soviet action whatever the cost. So, in 1979, President Jimmy Carter's administration shipped arms to the mujaheddin guerillas fighting the Soviet invasion. Thanks to CIA complicity, the Afghan rebels were able to use profits from selling heroin to purchase arms. The heroin business boomed, with the Afghan crop becoming the second largest in the world.

In 1996 the Taliban spiritual leader, Mullah Omar, announced that his government was anti-heroin, anti-hashish and anti-drugs, though in reality it only held true to the second of these declarations. As the Taliban famously banned education for women and pictures of any living creature, it is, of course, not surprising that anything to do with drugs was on their list of no-nos, and – again not surprisingly – Afghanistan under the Taliban had some of the toughest penalties for drugs use in the world. As regards the drugs production and export business, however, they showed uncharacteristic flexibility. The drugs trade was officially banned but in practice tolerated. In fact it was tolerated to

'OUR emphasis is 90 per cent Communism, 10 per cent drugs.'
– Frank McNeil, ex-US Ambassador to Costa Rica and Assistant Secretary of State in charge of intelligence operations

the extent that Afghanistan became the world market leader in opium production.

In 1996, at a meeting with the United Nations to discuss aid, the Taliban said that they could not stop Afghan opium production as it was based in territories beyond their control. In a way this was true, because the opposition militias fighting the Taliban were also funding themselves through poppy cultivation. In another way, though, they were lying. US satellite surveys showed the extent to which opium production soared throughout the 1990s in areas firmly under Taliban control. Each spring, huge areas of south and east Afghanistan were covered with red opium poppies. Some of this opium was processed into heroin and morphine base in small factories inside the country. Some was carried out on camel or donkey trains to heroin labs in the Khyber Pass on the Pakistani border. Ultimately, all this opium passed on to Europe and the USA.

The opium industry was the backbone of the Afghan economy under the Taliban. Taxes on opium production supplied vital revenue, and the trade was one of the few ways foreign currency could be brought into the country. What's more, in poverty-stricken, war-ravaged Afghanistan the opium poppy was by far the most lucrative crop available to farmers. Although price mark-ups along the trafficking

AFGHANISTAN'S annual income from the heroin trade was estimated to be around £30 million in the mid-1990s.

'THE basic fact that eluded these great geniuses was that it takes only 10 square miles of poppies to feed the entire American heroin market, and they grow everywhere.'
  – Myles Ambrose, one-time adviser to President Nixon

route meant that in the UK Afghan heroin sold for a price 2,000 times greater than the farmers had received for it, their income was nevertheless still high compared with average Afghan wages.

Following the overthrow of the Taliban, farmers were offered $300 an acre to destroy their opium fields. Not only was the money nothing compared to the regular income opium provided, but many of the growers were in hock to drugs gangs. If they took the money and destroyed their crops, the drugs gangs would take retribution and the farmers would pay with their lives. There has been some resistance to the policy of opium destruction.

Nevertheless, in 2001 Afghan opium production did fall drastically – from 3,656 tonnes to 74 tonnes. The reason was not an anti-drugs programme or even the post-September 11 war. Output fell because of a drought. As ever in drugs history, the result of shortage is that prices go up and the business looks more attractive than ever.

 ## The French connection

Today, around 80 per cent of heroin on its way to Britain is said to pass out of Afghanistan through Iran and then through Turkey. Back in the 1950s, most raw opium came from Turkey and passed through Marseilles on the notorious French Connection route.

Following World War Two, the mafia leader Lucky Luciano was mysteriously released from prison in the USA and deported to Italy. There, he found his home in Sicily was a useful mid-point between opium-growing countries such as Turkey and the heroin users of America. When the Italian government was nudged by the USA to crack down on drug-trafficking enterprises, Luciano moved his operation to Marseilles.

In Marseilles, the CIA feared that communists were taking over the docks. To help undermine any such moves, local Corsican criminals were put on the CIA payroll and soon ended up in control of the docks themselves. Luciano's heroin business benefited greatly. Between 1951 and 1973 the French Connection supplied around 80 per cent of the heroin on the streets of the USA. When Turkey got out of the opium business in the 1960s, production moved, thanks in no small part to Corsican family connections, to French Indo-China, or

TO help close down the French Connection, the Americans developed a heroin sniffer. This was a VW camper van equipped with a snorkel in its roof. This was attached to a machine capable of detecting the acetic anydrides used in manufacturing heroin. The van may not have sniffed out any heroin factories, but it did lead the American authorities to a salad dressing manufacturer.

the Golden Triangle. When subsequent managers of the Marseilles operation started selling their products in France as well as America, their heroin labs were closed down remarkably quickly.

 ## The Golden Triangle

Following defeat by Mao Tse-Tung's communist army, Chiang Kai-shek's Kuomintang National People's Party, the KMT, were driven out of China. Some retreated to the Shan province of Burma. From here the war with China was financed with proceeds from opium production. Like the Afghan rebels, the KMT received US backing and CIA arms and training. Also, as in Afghanistan, opium production was tolerated by the CIA as a means to raise funds for the struggle against the communists. Thanks to this, by the early 1960s Burma's opium production had risen from 15 to 300 tons a year.

In Laos in the early 1950s, French forces fought Ho Chi-Minh's communists. Again the drugs trade provided funds for the campaign thanks to an air link, established by the French and operated by their airforce, between Laos's poppy fields and Saigon's opium dens. Following French withdrawal in 1955, a few hundred veterans stayed behind. Some of these were French and some of them were our friends the Corsicans. Among the veterans were some trained as pilots, who set up charter airlines. Officially this was to transport businessmen, but the real business was moving opium to refineries in Thailand and Vietnam.

When, in 1958, a left-wing government was elected in Laos, America cut its aid and did not reinstate it until a more acceptable politician, Phoumi Nosova, took over leadership. When Phoumi refused to establish a coalition government in 1961, aid was cut again. So Phoumi turned to the opium trade for finance. Burmese opium was imported and Laos began to establish itself as one of the world's major heroin-producing centres.

As the Vietnam war developed, Laos's planes were used for bombing raids, and in 1965 the charter airlines set up by the Corsicans had their rights to land at airports removed. There was still, of course, a large amount of opium needing to be transported, so in order that the anti-communist forces were kept in business, transport planes intended for use by CIA operatives were used to carry opium.

Not only were the Americans supplying a vital service to the Burmese and Laotian drugs trade, they had also imported a ready market for the end product. It is estimated that by 1971 10–15 per cent of American servicemen in Vietnam were on heroin. For this reason the local drugs factories started to produce a higher class of product than the low-grade brown heroin that had been fine for the locals. By the end of the Vietnam war, south-east Asia was a major manufacturer of heroin to Western standards.

Throughout the 1980s and 1990s, the opium trade moved from Laos to Thailand and eventually to Burma – or Myanmar. Today, the Burmese rulers say their intention is to end opium production by 2005. In the meantime, opium is produced mainly in the remote hilly country near the border with China, by ethnic insurgents out of government control. The government has even granted autonomy to a group of them, called the Wa, formed from the remnants of Burma's communist party. The Wa's state within a state now has its own army and is entirely devoted to, and financed by, the drugs trade.

In the face of attempts to end opium production, the Wa have diversified. It is the Wa who produce the methamphetamine tablets known as yaba that are spreading panic through areas such as Thailand. *Yaba* is Thai for 'crazy medicine', though this form of methamphetamine was originally developed in Nazi Germany to help storm troopers fight more viciously and for longer. Thirty years ago it was legally available in Thailand and was sold at garages to truckers who used it, as so many amphetamines have been used before, to drive for longer without sleep. It is now said that in Thailand use of the drug has increased by 2,000 per cent over a few years, making it now more popular than heroin. It is estimated that around 800 million yaba tablets are being turned out each year in laboratories within the Wa's territory. Yaba is particularly dangerous because it makes the user feel supremely powerful and leads to them behaving in a potentially extremely violent manner either to themselves or to others. Nevertheless, surely even drug dealers will realise that a substance that makes its users kill themselves doesn't have too much long-term business appeal?

Cannabis roots

Most of Europe's marijuana originates in west Africa, while Morocco, in north Africa, is a major supplier of Europe's hashish. Around 2,000 tons of cannabis a year enters Europe from Morocco, passing along trafficking routes through Spain, Gibraltar and France.

Another big supplier of hashish in Europe is the Lebanon. During the Lebanese civil war, in the 1970s, 80s and 90s, the drugs trade was, as in so many places, a source of vital funds for the warring factions. In the 1960s, Maronite Christians started growing hashish in the Bekaa Valley in eastern Lebanon, as well as trafficking opium and heroin from Asia. As a result they earned money to arm themselves. The Muslim population followed suit. By 1975 the Christians had lost their drug trade monopoly, while Syria took control of the Bekaa Valley. During the 1980s the area moved into the even more profitable production of opiates.

According to Rachel Ehrenfeld, the author of *Narco Terrorism*, the PLO, under Yasir Arafat, made 'an official decision to use the drug trade to its advantage ... six months after its expulsion from Beirut'. Ehrenfeld has reported how the PLO's 'traffic in arms and drugs has been assisted by airport investments' in Nairobi and in Lagos, which provide 'a base for forged travel documents and airline tickets'.

 ## The coca cabana

South America is, famously, another major centre for the international business that is drugs. During the 1990s Peru was the main producer of coca in the world. The Peruvian coca business has, however, now shrunk by two-thirds. The reduction in business came about partly as a result of a government instruction that any aircraft heading towards the refining plants of Colombia should be shot down. Similarly in Bolivia, coca production was halved between 1997 and 1999 as a result of aggressive government-led measures to destroy production of the crop in the country. Unfortunately, this has not resulted in any overall reduction in world production of coca for one simple reason: Colombia.

Colombia now produces around 75 per cent of the world's cocaine. Ten years ago the country was not a major coca producer but was instead known as a refiner of coca harvested elsewhere in the Andes. Colombia's government is, of course, committed to ending the country's association with drugs. Unfortunately, as in Burma, vast areas of Colombia are in the hands of anti-government forces which finance themselves through drugs. The drugs business has also burgeoned in Colombia beyond cocaine. The country is now also a leading supplier of heroin to the US.

A saint among men

During the 1980s Medellin, the capital of Antioquia province in Colombia, became the centre of cocaine production. Medellin was traditionally a conservative town famed for its civic pride. Indeed, one local businessman went so far as to personally finance the provision of free medical and dental care to all the poor of the area, as well as the distribution of 5,000 toys every Christmas to the town's street children, and the building of a new local church. He had free food distributed every fortnight and paid for new homes for 500 of

Medellin's poorest families. The newly built housing settlement, or barrio, was named in honour of this saint among men: Barrio Pablo Escobar. Can you guess where he got his money from?

Pablo Escobar was born in 1949. According to legend, as a youth, Escobar made a living stealing gravestones, sanding off their inscriptions and selling them for re-use. Around 1978 Escobar got into discussions with Fabio Ochoa Vasquez, who was running an alcohol and electrical equipment smuggling operation. Escobar persuaded him to change to a more profitable line: cocaine.

A few years earlier, Chile had been the main cocaine refiner. In 1973 General Pinochet had seized power and appeased the US by handing over several leading Chilean traffickers. As a result, the remaining traffickers and refiners decided to head north and settle in Colombia. Colombia's cocaine business was also helped by the fact that in the early 1980s cocaine was becoming increasingly fashionable. Escobar and Ochoa's founding of what became known as the Medellin Cartel was therefore extremely well timed. Their associate, Carlos Lehder, oversaw the operation from a base in the Bahamas, where the Prime Minister Sir Lynden Pindling was alleged to have received large payments from

PABLO Escobar became not only the world's richest criminal, but (by 1987) he was also the 14th richest person in the entire world. In 1982 he was earning $500,000 a day; by a few years later his salary had doubled.

him. From the Bahamas Colombian cocaine began to flow up through Florida into the USA.

The Colombian government, however, weren't happy. The drugs business was undermining democracy. Since the 1970s the Colombian traffickers had been becoming increasingly violent. Under Escobar, the Medellin cartel's gangs murdered thousands.

In the early 1980s Colombia's justice minister, Rodrigo Lara, began to investigate. Escobar had gained election to Colombia's Congress in 1982, so providing himself with immunity from prosecution. Following Lara's investigations into earlier crimes with which he had been associated, Escobar was, however, disgraced and forced to resign from Congress.

The Colombian authorities went on to raid Tranquilandia, the largest cocaine laboratory in the world. Planes from the lab's private airstrip were impounded and its employees were arrested, but not before they had attempted to dump 14 tons of cocaine in an adjacent river.

The investigations into Escobar ended abruptly and somewhat inevitably. In 1984 Lara was murdered. The following year a judge concluded that Escobar had been involved in the murder. Shortly afterwards the judge was murdered. By now under threat of investigation and extradition, the cartel went on a rampage involving car bombs, the shooting of Lara's successor three times in the face, a bloody seige of the Bogota Palace of Justice and the murder of various newspaper editors and judges.

Escobar had become so distracted by the violence that another cartel, the Cali, had started to take his business. By

1987, when Escobar offered the Cali cartel the opportunity to merge with his operation, they were large enough and strong enough to be able to refuse.

Escobar's cohorts still went further. In 1989 the Governor of the Antioquia province and the region's chief of police were both murdered, and presidential candidate, Luis Carlos Galan, was assassinated in front of a crowd of his supporters. An aeroplane carrying 107 people from Bogota to Cali was blown up in an attempt to murder another presidential candidate.

Eventually the Colombian Constitutional Assembly announced that Escobar would not be extradited. This was the news he had been waiting for and so he handed himself in. He was imprisoned in a luxury penitentiary, built on land he had sold to the government himself. Essentially Escobar was imprisoned on a luxury estate which he owned. His prison included a gymnasium, a disco, a jacuzzi, a football pitch, accommodation for his henchmen and a field in which cannabis could be grown.

When the government threatened to put him in something that more resembled a prison, Escobar went on the run. With the government, the American authorities and the Cali cartel all contributing to the reward for his capture, it wasn't long before Escobar was run to ground. The end came because he did a newspaper interview. While answering questions over his mobile phone in December 1993, he was tracked down and killed. Thousands of others had also been killed along the way. All that over a bit of white powder. Escobar was still a hero to the poor of Medellin, however. Five thousand of them turned up at his funeral wanting to touch the body.

ONE method of laundering drugs money in 1980s and 90s Colombia was by channelling it through the football business. Six of Colombia's 14 main soccer teams were owned by drug traffickers. As a result of the money available, the national Colombian team reached the World Cup finals in 1994, the first time they had done so since 1962. Local football in Colombia was rife with corruption and match fixing, and it is rumoured that this was carried over into the World Cup. Andres Escobar (no relation to Pablo) scored an own goal in a vital match in the championships. Rumours that he did this on purpose have never been proved. Nevertheless, the goal cost Escobar his life. He was shot dead on his return to Colombia.

These days most coca production in Colombia takes place in the south of the country, in areas controlled by guerillas. As these guerillas are both leftist and drug dealers, the US had no hesitation in proposing military assistance to help Colombia crush them. The guerillas, of course, have their own view of matters and an attractively designed website (www.farc-ep.org).

INTO THE BODY

 Possession

We have seen that what was once taken in Europe and America to be demonic possession was probably caused by the accidental consumption of hallucinogenic ergot mould. Today in the West we are generally less worried about possession by evil spirits, but drugs seem to have taken their place as the demons of modern society. Drugs, apparently, are lurking everywhere, waiting to leap inside us and seize control at the first opportunity. Individuals possessed by drugs are reduced to zombie-like creatures wreaking devastation on the decent folk around them. Tabloid newspapers regularly describe addicts' case histories as 'a descent into hell' or 'a life in hell'. But how do drugs possess us? How do they work on our brains and bodies?

Hijacked

An article in the *New Scientist* magazine pointed out that 'addictive drugs share the ability to hijack a neural pathway in the brain ... that makes, eating, having sex and mothering infants seem pleasurable and worth repeating. In cold biological terms, the threat of addiction is the price we must pay for having evolved the capacity to respond to pleasure; or, if you like, for not being bored to death by sex and food.' So it seems drugs can have the effects they do because they resemble substances already present in our bodies.

Amphetamines, for example, resemble norepinephrine or noradrenaline, a naturally ocurring nerve impulse transmitter in the body. Norepinephrine was particularly important to our ancestors because it plays a role in the fight or flight response. Drugs like amphetamines and cocaine cause a lot of activity in the brain and spinal cord, mimicking and enhancing the action of norepinephrine in the brain. They thereby make you feel much more aroused and responsive to the world around you. Thus the experience of cocaine is usually an intensification of the body's normal stimulatory mechanisms. A bit like being alive but more so.

Designed for opiates

In the early 1970s researchers at John Hopkins University, USA, studying the workings of the human brain made a remarkable discovery. According to their findings, not only did human beings enjoy taking opiate drugs but they had

THE term endorphin is in fact an abbreviation of 'endogenous morphine'. It might as well have been called 'self-produced heroin'.

been designed to take them. Studies of the human brain showed that it seemed to be tailor-made to receive and enjoy drugs such as morphine and heroin.

The scientists had identified receptor sites in the brain. These sites are cells, lying in the middle region of the brain, that govern the response to pain. They do this by reacting with chemicals that arrive through the bloodstream to bind with them. If the right chemical arrives, the system reacts in such a way that less pain is felt. The receptor sites found by the John Hopkins team allowed only one type of chemical to bind with them – the type found in opiate drugs.

Was the ultimate purpose of human existence now clear? Had human beings either evolved or been designed for the ultimate purpose of taking heroin? Further research soon showed that this was not quite the case. What the brain cell receptor sites were supposed to receive was neurotransmitters called endorphins. Neurotransmitters are the means by which messages are transferred between neurons in the brain. In other words, they help pass on the information that lets you know whether what you're experiencing is pleasurable, painful or whatever. Endorphins are the neurotransmitters that help deal with pain. Guess what. Opiates are chemically very similar to endorphins.

The body's natural endorphins are designed to trigger the

brain's receptor sites. Once triggered, the receptor sites send out chemicals to relieve the pain of injury or exertion. This is the high that people experience after hard exercise. When heroin triggers the same receptor sites, the effect is to create a warm, pain-free sensation. This is all very nice if life is generally difficult and painful. Unfortunately, along the way heroin kills not only all pain but also all feeling.

Heroin is particularly dangerous because it is very fast-acting, especially when mainlined. Intravenous use of heroin gets 68 per cent of the drug into the brain as against 5 per cent of morphine. Also, as heroin is more soluble in fat cells, it can cross the blood–brain barrier in 15 to 20 seconds, which accounts for the rush that heroin users experience.

Cannabis on the brain

Cannabis affects the frontal cortex of the brain – the region that governs activities such as decision-making, social skills and high level consciousness – to create dreaminess and euphoria. It also tends to suppress cell firing in a region of the brain called the hippocampus which governs information storage and retrieval. Hence, then, dope's notorious effect on

THE sociologist John Auld has argued that the effects of cannabis are a learned experience. In other words, new users of the drug have to learn what they are supposed to feel. This is apparently the reason why many first-time cannabis users feel nothing and wonder what all the fuss is about.

memory. Recently scientists have succeeded in identifying the brain receptor site that is hit by cannabis's main psychoactive cannabinoid ingredient, delta-9-tetrahydro-cannabinol or THC). They do not yet definitely know, however, which naturally occurring neurotransmitter is intended to react with this site – a neurotransmitter that THC must presumably resemble in some way.

Vitamin K

While drugs like heroin can provide a pain-free bubble in which the user can escape all the world's problems, keta-mine can kill the sensation of pain, though it works in a very different way. Ketamine is a disassociative anaesthetic. Unlike normal painkilling drugs, ketamine doesn't slow the body down, it speeds it up. The way it stops the brain regis-tering pain is by blocking normal thinking completely. Left in a vacuum, the brain cannot see, hear or sense anything. It loses awareness even of the body in which it resides. So, in the absence of anything else to do, it creates its own reality out of memories, dreams and fantasies.

Hallucinogens and serotonin

The compounds found in hallucinogens such as ergot have been discovered to be similar to serotonin. Serotonin is another neurotransmitter released by nerve cells in the brain and is thought to play a role in controlling mood and regu-lating memory, sleep patterns, perception of pain, appetite, libido and emotion. Ergot reduces the natural production of serotonin. The serotonin receptor sites compensate for this by increasing their sensitivity to whatever serotonin is left. They then get hit instead by large amounts of serotonin-like hallucinogens. The result is dramatic mood swings and hallucinations.

Ecstasy on the other hand is a stimulant that increases brain activity and causes a massive release of serotonin. (Prozac, similarly, works by raising serotonin levels.) Ecstasy prevents nerve cells absorbing serotonin, and so high concentrations are left in the brain and body tissues. The feelings of tiredness, irritability and inability to think straight known as the 'ecstasy hangover' are thought to result from the depletion of serotonin that ultimately occurs.

Research has suggested that ecstasy also damages the nerves that release serotonin – and once these serotonin pathways are damaged, they can never repair themselves. The result could be long-term memory disturbance and depression, with users feeling as if permanently jet-lagged. Men and women, however, seem to respond differently to low serotonin levels. Women become depressed, while men behave more aggressively.

An autopsy of a 26-year-old Canadian who had been a long-term heavy user of ecstasy suggested that the drug had had a significant effect. His brain contained between 50 per cent and 80 per cent less serotonin than it should have done. How seriously these problems will affect the 2 million or so people who take ecstasy in the UK, we should begin to find out in a few years' time.

Ecstasy and football hooliganism

Ecstasy is said to be one possible explanation for the down-turn in some hooliganism and violence in recent years. In his book *E for Ecstasy*, Nicholas Saunders describes how, in the summer of 1992, 'many of the hard core lads, who had previously been beating each other up, had spent most of the summer dancing the weekends away to the sound of house music at raves fuelled by the drug ecstasy'.

Saunders also describes how, in November of the same year, the day before Manchester United were due to play Manchester City in a local derby match, two gangs of rival supporters met in a club 'after necking an E'. The mayhem that might have been expected did not transpire and a member of one of the gangs noted, 'Well, who'd have thought that we would be stood side by side the night before a derby game, and there's no trouble in any of us? It's weird innit? It could never have happened before E.'

There again, the 1960s era of peace and love in music came to an abrupt end at the Rolling Stones show in Altamont, California when poor quality LSD resulted in violence and the fatal stabbing of Meredith Hunter. At the next World Cup maybe everyone will be on yaba.

Who put the dope in the dopamine?

While endorphins are involved in feelings of pain relief and pleasure, they in turn stimulate another chemical in the body known as dopamine or the dopamine system. Dopamine is a

HEROIN, cocaine, alcohol and nicotine all trigger dopamine in one small mid-brain structure called the nucleus accumbens. Many regard the ability to stimulate this area as being the hallmark of an addictive substance.

neurotransmitter related to adrenalin. One particular complex of nerves where dopamine is produced seems to be of enormous importance in the way the human body experiences pleasure. Dopamine is perhaps, then, the body's natural 'happy juice'.

Many psychoactive drugs ultimately stimulate the dopamine system even if their effect is initially felt elsewhere. Alcohol, for example, works at first on other transmitters but eventually stimulates dopamine. PCP, or angel dust, works initially on the body's glutimate system but, again, ultimately affects levels of dopamine. Methamphetamine, or yaba, also causes the brain to flood with dopamine, causing huge exhilaration followed by terrible lows. Cannabis also increases dopamine production, while opiates, such as morphine and heroin, ultimately stimulate its release. The result is a feeling of intense euphoria and the, perhaps misguided, bodily sensation that these are exceptionally good substances to take.

Dopamine itself is found in the areas of the brain that deal with emotion. If you can get some dopamine washing round your bloodstream, you feel good and life seems worthwhile. In biochemical terms, dopamine is the reward sent out to tell us that something is worth doing. So having sex and eating food both stimulate the dopamine system, with the result that you feel pleasure and satisfaction.

These days human beings have found lots of ways to stimulate dopamine and, strictly speaking, a lot of these don't really help with the survival of the species. Eating a bar of chocolate or drinking a cold beer, for example, can increase your dopamine levels. Unfortunately, these dopamine hits don't last for very long. The body doesn't normally allow you to have dopamine floating around for too long. Instead, it sweeps it up so that it can be recycled for another time. What would happen, though, if you had a drug that could stop dopamine being cleared away? You could have more and more dopamine washing round your system. Think how good you'd feel then. Such a product is available. It's called cocaine.

 ## Cocaine on the brain

In some ways, cocaine gets the dopamine system going in the same way as other drugs. It gets dopamine into your system, which makes you feel good. Then it does what other drugs fail to. It stops dopamine being mopped up for recycling. Cocaine hits a molecule called the dopamine transporter and disables it. So less dopamine is taken away for reuse and more is left in your system. So you end up feeling better than ever, awash with dopamine.

This may sound great but, as with so many things in life, it doesn't stay great for long. As comedian Jeremy Hardy warned about people who have sex too often, the problem

PROZAC, which became the most widely prescribed anti-depressant in history, belongs to a class of drugs known as selective serotonin re-uptake inhibitors, or SSRIs. Like the other SSRIs Zoloft, Paxil and Luvox, Prozac works by increasing brain levels of the neurotransmitter sero-tonin, which is thought to influence sleep, appetite, aggression and mood. Prozac works on serotonin much as cocaine acts on dopamine: it inhibits the re-uptake of serotonin – in other words, it gets increased levels of serotonin into the system by preventing it from being re-absorbed. For reasons as yet not entirely understood, this increase in serotonin levels reduces feelings of depression.

Prozac has been accused of having various side-effects, including headaches, nausea, delayed orgasm and an increased tendency to suicidal thoughts – although probably not all at once. As doctors have pointed out, however, many of the so-called side-effects may actually be symptoms of the original psychological problem. For example, a depressed person who takes Prozac and then has suicidal thoughts may be having those suicidal thoughts as a result of the depression rather than because of the Prozac.

is you use up your goes. People who use a lot of cocaine ultimately end up with less dopamine in their bodies; indeed, after just three months of cocaine use, there will be abnor-mally low levels of dopamine in circulation. The whole natu-ral pleasure system has been run down. Now things that would previously have caused pleasure don't have much effect at all.

Addiction

At some point when drugs such as heroin are being taken over time, a change occurs that is difficult to reverse. Now, instead of taking the drug to enhance feelings of pleasure, the addict requires drugs to feel any pleasure whatsoever. The brain's whole natural chemistry can, for example, be usurped by morphine, which is what heroin changes to in the blood. Now the opiate drugs, or the imposter endorphins, are the only endorphins you've got.

Studies have also shown that intensive cocaine use hijacks body chemistry. It is known that dopamine levels in cocaine addicts leap before they take the drug. If the cocaine isn't delivered into the system, they then suffer an excruciating craving. Protracted use of cocaine also tends to reorder the brain's natural circuitry. Activities such as eating and

'COCAINE habit forming? Of course not. I ought to know, I've been using it for years.'

– Tallulah Bankhead

IT appears that many people are able to take drugs without becoming addicted. A 1974 study of GIs returning from the Vietnam war who had used heroin regularly while involved in the conflict showed that once back in the USA they were able to stop their regular heroin use without too much difficulty. Some continued to use heroin on occasion but without becoming addicted.

having sex are normally hardwired as prime goals, but in cocaine addicts these normal motivations are knocked from the top slot by the goal of taking more cocaine.

 ## What's gone wrong?

Some drug users end up in a situation where they're no longer taking drugs to feel pleasure at all. They're taking them to stop themselves from feeling terrible. How can this be if drugs stimulate pleasure-promoting dopamine?

In one set of tests, animals were offered drugs that had been specially treated to block the dopamine system. No dopamine, no pleasure. The animals understandably refused to take these drugs. Next, the scientists got the animals hooked on some regular pleasure-promoting drugs. Once they were addicted, the scientists took the drugs away. The animals were then once again given the treated drugs that blocked the dopamine system. Now that the animals were hooked, the fact that the drugs didn't work on the dopamine system didn't matter any more. They took them anyway. So eventually users seem to move on from taking drugs for the benefit of getting pleasurable dopamine into their systems to taking them for some other reason.

Only 5 to 10 per cent of hard drug users become addicted. Clearly, issues such as the quantity of drugs that are taken, the frequency with which they're taken, how rapidly they're taken and the general mental state of the individual concerned are all involved in whether addiction develops or not. Of addicts undergoing treatment to get them off drugs, between 50 and 80 per cent relapse. One of the significant problems is that the act of coming off drugs doesn't mean that the craving for them gradually goes away. It does the opposite. If an addict manages to avoid drugs for a few months but then comes into contact with things likely to make him feel like taking them again, his brain will be even more responsive to these stimuli than if he were still a regular user.

SOME physical effects of drugs are entirely due to the weird workings of individual brains.

A medical intern reported having treated 'a middle-aged, slightly dishevelled hippy' suffering from FBIP, or Foreign Body In Penis. After smoking a few joints the individual concerned had decided to see what would happen 'if he snaked a three-foot length of aquarium tubing into his penis'. He managed to get all but 15 centimetres (6 inches) in. Then he discovered it was more difficult to get it back out again. To try and help sort things out, he threaded wire 'from a Weed Wacker' through the centre of the tubing. This in turn became stuck. So he gave up for the day and went to bed.

A night's sleep failed to shift the problem and now he found 'he had trouble doing his gardening with tubing hanging out of his penis'. So he cut the tubing flush with his skin. Eventually he was brought into hospital. His initial self-diagnosis that he had some tube and some wire stuck up his penis was confirmed. X-rays showed that they had become knotted in his bladder. A urologist somehow managed to get a scope up through the, by now, overcrowded urethra, cut the knot and released the tubing.

To combat this problem, vaccines for cocaine and nicotine addiction are now said to be in development. It is anticipated that such vaccines would bind like antibodies to drugs entering the body's system and prevent them from acting on the brain. Whether the development of such products would be of financial interest to major pharmaceutical companies remains debatable. It is also debatable whether they would be used to treat people with existing addictions or people identified as likely to develop them. The history of anti-addiction drugs does not, however, give great cause for optimism. Two products were championed in the 19th century as cures for morphine addiction. One was cocaine and the other was heroin.

SURELY NOT ON DRUGS ...

 Astronauts

Apollo astronauts were reported to have used amphetamines to promote the endurance they required to handle re-entry into Earth's atmosphere following space missions. In 1981 it was reported that, 'On the maiden flight of the shuttle in April, rookie astronaut Robert Crippen avoided the queasies by dipping into the medical kit for a NASA-developed prescription of Dexedrine, a stimulant, and scopolamine, a tranquilizer.' At the same time, Soviet cosmonauts were using ginseng.

 Marion Barry

Mayor of Washington from 1978 to 1990, Barry was first accused of using cocaine at a nightclub in 1983 and was subsequently caught on video by the FBI smoking crack cocaine with a female acquaintance who had 'agreed to work with the federal authorities'. Barry was arrested in January 1990. At his trial he admitted that he did on occasion use cocaine. The jury was deeply and passionately divided on the case, some feeling that the government was 'out to get Marion Barry', but he was finally convicted on a charge of possession of cocaine. This was one of 14 charges that had been brought against him. He was sentenced to six months in prison as well as a $5,000 fine. Amazingly, he was re-elected mayor in 1994.

 ## George W. Bush

Allegations of drug use by the current US president were made in a 1999 book entitled *Fortunate Son* but remain completely unproven. Nevertheless, when asked whether he has ever used illegal drugs, Bush has consistently and vehemently evaded the subject. In the 1994 Texas governor's race, the *Houston Chronicle* asked him if he had ever taken drugs and received the reply, 'Maybe I did, maybe I didn't. ... How I behaved as an irresponsible youth is irrelevant to this campaign.' In response to a similar question from *Scotland on Sunday*, Bush declared, 'When I was young and irresponsible, I was young and irresponsible.' In the 1999 presidential campaign, Bush was able proudly to tell the *Dallas Morning News* that he could pass the standard background check for federal employees. This check asked, among other questions, whether an applicant had used illegal drugs within the past seven years. So Bush was prepared to state categorically that he had not used illegal drugs since 1992. Later, he went further and said he could have passed the same examination when his father became president in 1989. An aide enthusiastically joined in this gradual pushing back of the 'definitely drugs-free period' by telling the press that Bush had not used illegal drugs in at least the last 25 years. So President Bush's life is divided into two parts. The past 25 years or so, when we are told he has definitely not used any illegal drugs, and the period before that, when he doesn't admit anything.

 ## Bill Clinton

US president from 1993 to 2000, Clinton famously smoked cannabis but 'did not inhale' while at Oxford University in the 1960s. Surprisingly, once he was elected president his youthful non-inhaling experiences did not lead to any leniency towards other dope users, whether they had inhaled or not. In his first year as president, 380,399 Americans were arrested for crimes related to marijuana. In 1999, his final year in office, this figure had risen by around 85 per cent, to 704,812.

 ## Clive of India

Robert Clive, 18th-century British soldier and administrator, was sent to sort things out in India following the Patna massacre. Once he was in control, he used the trade in Indian opium to help fund needed reforms. Clive was an opium user himself, and died in 1774 after taking a double dose of the drug.

Anthony Eden

Eden, British prime minister from 1955 to 1957, reportedly 'lived on benz', i.e. Benzedrine amphetamine, during the crisis caused by the Egyptian seizure of the Suez Canal in 1956.

Benjamin Franklin

The 18th-century US statesman, author and scientist. Franklin started one of America's first paper mills using cannabis hemp. The paper mill was therefore able to work without dependence on imports of foreign supplies.

Hermann Goering

Founder of the Gestapo and Marshal of the Reich under Hitler, in 1939 Hermann Goering could have been Nazi slimmer of the year. He lost 18 kilograms (40 pounds) in just two months. It is presumed that amphetamines, or perhaps cocaine, were used to assist with this crash diet. It is also known that Goering was addicted to morphine and was taking up to 100 paracodeine pills a day during the time of the Nuremberg trials.

Al Gore

Gore, vice-president to Bill Clinton, admitted occasional marijuana use during his 1960's college years and while serving the US military in Vietnam.

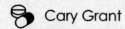 Cary Grant

Cary Grant, the British-born Hollywood star of the 1940s and 50s, took LSD more than 60 times and declared that acid had given him what yoga, hypnotism and mysticism had all failed to provide: 'Peace of mind'. He took LSD with his doctor sitting alongside him to offer words of guidance during his trips, and in his autobiography promoted the drug enthusiastically while mourning its recently established illegality: 'For a slow learner, I learned a great deal ... and the result of it all was rebirth. A new assessment of life and myself in it. An immeasurably beneficial cleansing of so many needless fears and guilts, and a release of the tensions that had been the result of them.'

 King George IV

George IV reigned in Great Britain from 1820 to 1830. The Duke of Wellington observed of him, 'He drinks spirits morning, noon and night; and he is obliged to take laudanum to calm the irritation which the use of spirits occasions.'

 William Gladstone

British prime minister 1868–74, 1880–85, 1886 and 1892–94, Gladstone took laudanum in his coffee to increase his rhetorical abilities during speeches to Parliament.

John Hervey, Marquess of Bristol

John Hervey, the 7th Marquess of Bristol, died in 1999, aged 44, of a 'flu-like bug' after a lifetime of drink and drug abuse. The marquess inherited £1 million at the age of 16, and then, at the age of 18, another £4 million. At first, shrewd investment on his part helped increase his fortune, but when he inherited his father's estate in 1985, he proceeded to fritter it away on drugs, cars, drink and sex. After imprisonment for smuggling cocaine into Jersey in the late 1980s, he was jailed for a second time in 1993 for heroin and cocaine possession. During his trial it was revealed that his spending on drugs had cost his family over £7 million in less than 10 years. A raid by the drugs squad in 1991 uncovered drugs hidden in Herveys' old master paintings, in a gold Russian snuff box and in a can of Pledge furniture polish. His half-sister is London society girl and model, Lady Victoria Hervey, whose younger brother has now inherited the title (minus the property) of Marquess of Bristol.

Adolf Hitler

Every morning Hitler's physician Dr Theo Morell would give the Führer a 'vitamin shot'. Before receiving this boost Hitler was said to be extremely lethargic. Afterwards, as Himmler noted, he perked up a treat and became alert, active and ready to go about his business. The shots were almost certainly amphetamines, and as the war progressed Adolf started increasing the dose to between two and five injections a day. Adolf's 'vitamin shots' were alternated with tablets including Pervitin, which was a commercial brand of methamphetamine. Dr Morrell is said to have administered at least 92 different drugs to the Führer during World War Two. These included strychnine, belladonna, morphine, hypnotics and aphrodisiacs. Following the assassination attempt of July 1944, Adolf developed a sore throat and was treated by Doctor Erwin Giesing, who administered cocaine in 10 per cent solutions. This was so effective that the treatment was continued well after the sore throat got better.

Adolf may also have had a drug named after him. The synthetic drug methadone hydrochloride, now used to wean users off heroin and on to a different highly addictive substance, was first formulated in Nazi Germany. Its creators originally gave it the name Dolophine Hydrochloride, possibly as a tribute to Hitler.

 ## Sherlock Holmes

Sherlock Holmes, the fictional detective created by Arthur Conan Doyle, is depicted in various stories as being an intravenous cocaine user. The first literary depiction of his cocaine taking is in the 1886 story 'Scandal in Bohemia'. Dr Watson describes Holmes as 'alternating from week to week between cocaine and ambition', injecting himself three times a day for three months and having arms that are 'all dotted and scarred with innumerable puncture marks'. Perhaps significantly, Conan Doyle had studied medicine at Edinburgh University, where his tutor had been Sir Robert

Christison, who had spent the 1870s experimenting with coca during mountain-climbing expeditions.

Thomas Jefferson

Jefferson was US president from 1801 to 1808. Like George Washington before him, he grew hemp on his plantations.

John F. Kennedy (and Jackie)

As well as shots of steroids and painkillers to combat Addison's disease, Kennedy (US president 1961–63) is also reported to have received regular injections of methyl-amphetamine. This treatment lasted apparently until his death and was administered by Max 'Dr Feelgood' Jacobson, a notorious 'doctor to the stars'. Jacobson provided amphetamine shots not only to President Kennedy but also to first lady, Jackie Kennedy. According to the *New York Times*, JFK was warned by another of his doctors that 'No President with his finger on the red button has any business taking stuff like that.'

Popes Leo XIII and Pius X

Among the many 19th-century celebrities to whom Angelo Mariani sent samples of his coca-infused Vin Mariani wine to for endorsement was Pope Leo XIII. In January 1898 Mariani received in return for his efforts a papal gold medal together with a special message:

His Holiness has deigned me to thank the distin-
guished donor in his holy name, and to demonstrate
His gratitude in a material way as well. His Holiness
does me the honour of presenting Mr Mariani with a
gold medal containing His venerable coat of arms.

When Pope Pius X was appointed in 1903, it wasn't long
before he, too, received a cocaine-infused present. Pius X
responded:

His Holiness has received the bottle of coca wine sent
by Signor Mariani. This indication of your devoted
respect has been really welcomed by His Holiness,
who has asked me to let His pleasure be known to
yourself and ask you at the same time to thank the
same donor in name of His Holiness Himself. I am sure
you will be eager to fulfil such a high wish.

Abraham Lincoln

Records of the young Lincoln's account at Corneau & Diller's
drugstore in Springfield between 1855 and 1861 show that
the future US president purchased brandy, liniment containing
hemlock and laudanum, and three sticks of 25 cent cough
candy containing opium. It has also been claimed that Lincoln
bought a 50 cent bottle of cocaine in October 1860. As this
was over 20 years before Sigmund Freud tried to popularise
the drug in Europe, it is likely that the druggist's reference to
'cocoaine' could have indicated a coca-based product such

as coca wine or, even more likely, a coconut-based hair tonic called 'Cocoaine' on sale at the time in 50 cent bottles.

 ## Isaac Newton

English physicist and mathematician Isaac Newton supposedly had an alchemical garden at his Cambridge lodgings in which, as well as presumably discovering gravity when the apple dropped on his head, he grew cannabis, opium and other psychoactive herbs.

 ## Florence Nightingale

A 19th-century British hospital reformer, Florence Nightingale is famous for her work as a nurse tending British troops in the Crimean War, where she became known as 'the lady with the lamp'. On her return, perhaps 'the lady with the lumps' might have been more appropriate, as she became an intravenous drug user. This was possibly to counteract the psychological effects of no longer working and also to combat back pain. 'Nothing did me any good,' she said, 'but a curious little new-fangled operation of putting opium under the skin which relieves one for 24 hours.'

 ## Lord Rosebery

Lord Rosebery, a late 19th-century British prime minister, used a sleeping drug called Sulfonal to help ease the pressures of office. He also took to using cocaine as a means to pep up his public appearances. The solicitor general in Rosebery's government, Sir Frank Lockwood, was more brazen still in his drug-taking. Lockwood sat injecting himself with morphine in the House of Commons itself.

William Shakespeare

In 2001, 24 clay pipe fragments excavated from New Place, the final home of William Shakespeare in Stratford-upon-Avon, and other sites nearby were tested to establish what had been smoked in them. The results showed that some of these 17th-century pipes contained nicotine, cocaine, a hallucinogenic substance called myristic acid and possibly cannabis. *Cannabis sativa* was definitely used in Shakespeare's time to make hemp products. These products included not only the ropes and sails needed by Raleigh, Drake and Britain's other seafarers but also the paper used to print the King James Bible and Shakespeare's works. Portuguese travellers in India and European explorers in southern Africa were already aware of the use of hallucinogenic hemp in the 16th century, and coca chewing had been observed by the Spanish in South America. Contemporary records do not, however, give any suggestion that coca or cannabis were ever used, like tobacco, in a pipe smoking mixture. It is also incredibly unlikely that the pipe fragments studied ever belonged to Shakespeare himself, and even less likely that those found to contain cocaine did, as they were not among the fragments found at his house. Despite references in the sonnets to a 'noted weed', 'compounds strange' and 'a journey in his head', and the suggestions made by several excitable newspapers following the pipe study, there is no evidence that Shakespeare took drugs.

Homer Simpson

In the *Simpsons* episode 'El Viaje Misterioso de Nuestro Jomer', Homer visits the Springfield Chilli Cook Off ('please lick spoons clean after each use'). There, after eating a chilli pepper laced by Chief Wiggum with 'the merciless peppers of Quetzlzacatenango', he begins to have a weird hallucination involving a pyramid and a mystical coyote. The coyote sends Homer on a quest to seek out his soul mate. As Marge does not at first accept Homer's excuse for his behaviour at the chilli cook off ('Oh, honey, I didn't get drunk. I just went to a strange fantasy world'), it takes some wandering and soul searching for the pair eventually to become reconciled.

Queen Victoria

Ruler of Great Britain and of the British Empire 1837–1901, Queen Victoria was prescribed cannabis by her physician, John Reynolds, who described it as 'one of the most powerful medicines we possess'. Victoria used it to relieve period pains.

George Washington

While Washington was US president (1789–96), hemp was grown on plantations in his possession. Don't forget, though, hemp was once seen as a vital resource in America, and laws were passed ordering farmers to grow it. Hemp was even used to pay for goods and taxes.

William Wilberforce

Wilberforce was a British politician and campaigner against the slave trade, which was ended, thanks to his work, a month after his death by the 1833 Slavery Abolition Act. He was also an opium addict. In 1788, he was prescribed the drug for ulcerative colitis. Thirty years later he was still taking a pill of 4 grains of opium three times a day.

OUT OF THEIR TINY MINDS

Animals on Drugs

 ## His master's vice

It's a well-known fact that if you live with someone who has a drug habit you may well end up taking drugs yourself. Unfortunately, it seems that this rule applies even if you are an animal and the drug user is your owner.

From Fat Freddy's Cat in the *Fabulous Furry Freak Brothers* onwards, it doesn't take too much imagination to guess just what's going to happen if you place a small furry creature in the care of a bored recreational drug user. So, during the 1960s, Syd Barrett's manager, Peter Jenner, surely hadn't thought things through when he got the spaced-out Pink Floyd leader to look after his pet cat for him. And, indeed, it wasn't too long before the unfortunate moggy found itself being fed not on the Cattomeat he was expecting but with a spoonful of Uncle Syd's special medicine. 'He fed the cat acid,' commented Jenner later, as if any other outcome to the proceedings had been remotely possible.

This kind of animal abuse, though, isn't confined to stoned hippies from the 1960s. Many today are still risking simultaneous raids from the drugs squad and the animal cruelty inspectors. Indeed, with moves to relax Britain's drug laws, the situation seems increasingly to be coming out into the open. In January 2002, a Blackpool vet, Romain Pizzi, made an appeal through the pages of the *Veterinary Record* to find out if his colleagues were experiencing the increase in the sort of enquiries he had observed.

It seemed that a growing number of owners were becoming concerned that their pets were on something, and it wasn't heat. The *Guardian* newspaper interviewed Pizzi as he treated his latest small furry victim of accidental poisoning, 'a chilled-out chinchilla'. Brought in for a check-up after it had consumed what its owner gallantly named as some of his teenage son's cannabis ('It's never their own,' noted the vet), the chinchilla turned out to be suffering only minimal effects.

'The animal was anorexic and mildly depressed,' commented Pizzi. 'But it can cause coma and even death in some animals. It depends on the species.' The chinchilla regained normal health in a week, after a prescription of fluids and antibiotics. Mr Pizzi voiced the opinion that the easing of the official line on cannabis meant that such cases were these days being presented to vets 'for what they truly are'.

Two hundred years ago in England, opium was intentionally given to animals as a form of sedative. People purchas-

IN Laos secondary smoking of heroin has been known to turn both cats and dogs into addicts. Tame macaque monkeys in India became regular users through their habit of licking out cold opium pipes.

ing laudanum in 19th-century Wisbech in Cambridgeshire, claimed it wasn't for their own use but rather for their pigs. 'They fat better when they're kept from crying,' reasoned the good folk of Wisbech as they purchased class A drugs for their porkers. Opium was also used in the 19th century in cattle medicine and to dope unmanageable horses. A child was recorded as having died as a result of drinking laudanum that had been intended for a calf.

Cool for cats

Some animals don't need to be forced into chemical indulgence. Cats even have a drug of their very own, one which is willingly supplied to them by owners the world over – catnip. Cat lovers everywhere will confirm that the plant catnip, otherwise known as catmint or *Nepeta cataria*, gets their pussy going. Possibly cats like catnip because it is a natural painkiller and helps to protect them against insect parasites. Nevertheless, their enthusiasm for the substance is intense. They will first sniff and lick the plant before moving on to chewing the leaves. They can then be seen to break off suddenly and stare blankly into space. They then rub themselves against the plant with their chin and cheek before doing a forward roll and rubbing their entire body against it.

THE Japanese pleasure plant matatabi contains similar active ingredients to catnip. Concentrated matatabi was offered to some of the big cats in Osaka Zoo in Japan. The cats were soon hooked on the substance and would break off from eating, drinking and even sex to sniff matatabi.

Some cats even seem to chase imaginary mice while under the influence.

Ronald K. Siegel describes the stages of the cat's ecstastic reaction to catnip as usually occurring over a period of about 10 minutes. Catnip, in fact, contains volatile oils called nepetalactones which are similar to the chemicals found in tomcat urine. Nevertheless, catnip appeals to both male and female cats. Concentrated extracts of catnip have even more of an effect and cause felines to twitch and salivate while showing signs of growing sexual excitement.

 ## Animal medicine and booze

And it's not just cats. It is now accepted that many animals seek out plants for their medicinal drug properties. In Tanzania, leaves from the aspilia plant are used by local herbalists to treat stomach ache and gut parasites. Chimpanzees in the same area also seem to be aware of the leaves' antibacterial chemical action and use them, along with other types of hairy-leaved plants, to cleanse their digestive systems.

Other animals have definitely progressed on to alcohol. African elephants come running over 10 kilometres (6 miles) for a taste of the intoxicating fermenting fruit of the marula tree. Indian elephants will raid illicit stills and then rampage drunk through villages. Similarly, vervet monkeys, on the Caribbean island of St Kitts, raid local bars for swigs of rum from glasses or bottles left unattended. Bohemian waxwings are known to stupefy themselves on rowan berries, sometimes to the extent that alcohol-ridden, liver-diseased birds are found dead in piles on the ground having literally fallen off their perches. However, the story that koala bears become intoxicated as a result of their diet of eucalyptus leaves is a myth. Although koalas sleep for 18 hours a day, this is a natural part of their lifestyle and not a result of wrecking themselves on intoxicating foliage.

 ## A dose of one millipede

In Madagascar, lemurs have been observed holding millipedes between their lips, gently biting them to make them angry and then rolling the bugs over their fur. South American capuchins do the same thing. When millipedes are attacked they protect themselves by exuding lethal chemicals such as benzoquinone and hydrogen cyanide. Lemurs may be using the millipedes as tiny tubes of ointment to fumigate themselves against mosquitoes and other parasites.

Like the cats with their catnip, however, the lemurs seem to enjoy the whole process more than might be thought normal for an insecticidal fur bath. In fact, after the effects of a millipede, the lemurs start to drool and show the trance-like effects of narcotic-induced intoxication for 20 minutes or so.

The capuchins in South America even share the creepy crawlies, and can be seen sitting in groups passing around a potent millipede.

 ## Sheep, jaguars, snails and the fight against crime

Bighorn sheep in the Canadian Rockies have been seen risking serious injury in their efforts to get to growths of narcotic lichen.

In the Amazon, jaguars are also known to be very partial to the vine used to make ayahuasca, which is chewed by the shamans of the Tukano tribes to gain the ability to communicate with animal spirits and even to turn into animals. The jaguar is a favourite incarnation, as it is believed to be an intermediary between the everyday world and the world of spirits. If the Tukano shaman do turn into jaguars, their tastes don't change too much.

The cocaine-producing coca plant is known to be enjoyed by birds, who eat the seeds. Insects including ants, beetles, moth larvae, aphids, mites and leafhoppers, on the other hand, seem to prefer the leaves. Surprisingly though, the stimulating powers of the coca plant have been observed to have their most noticeable effect on an unexpected creature:

'In one of the outdoor patches we found several coca plants that had been attacked by garden snails, a common pest in California backyards,' reported Ronald K. Siegel:

> *By now I was very familiar with snail behaviour and I immediately recognised that these were no ordinary*

A SNIFFER dog taken to Ilfracombe Community College in Devon in early 2002 certainly took her job seriously. The dog, Bonnie, had only been brought along as a prop for a police presentation to pupils about the dangers of drugs. Nevertheless, as the boys and girls filed out of the school hall after the talk, Bonnie took the opportunity to point out a group of them as possible users. Sure enough, Bonnie's owner then made a small seizure of cannabis from the school lockers and four boys were arrested. What better end could there possibly be for a drugs talk at school than a real life raid and arrest?

snails. They seemed stimulated and were feeding on the coca leaves in broad daylight, a most brazen act for these nocturnal creatures ... I found that the coca-fed snails would climb a glass rod in about 90 seconds, whereas those snails fed on ordinary garden ivy did it in about 120 seconds.

Customs officers have to take care that their dogs don't become addicted as a result of the consignments of chemicals they sniff out. 'Our dogs enjoy their work. To them it's all a game. They never become addicted to drugs,' solemnly declaims the official website of the British customs service. 'They search for the fun of it and know that if they find a scent they have been trained to detect they will be rewarded by their handler through play.'

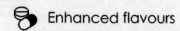

Enhanced flavours

Cheech and Chong can't have been the only two hippies to have enjoyed something akin to the following experience featured in their movie *Up In Smoke*:

> *'Man, what kinda shit is this man, I ain't never smoked no shit like that before, man!'*
>
> *'Well, it's supposed to be Maui Waui, but it's mostly Labrador.'*
>
> *'Labrador? What the hell is Labrador?'*
>
> *'I left my stash on the table man, and the little fucker ate it, man. I had to follow him around with a pooper scooper for a week, man.'*
>
> *'You mean we're smokin' dog shit, man? ... I wonder what Great Dane tastes like?'*

Consuming the drug-imbued excreta of animals is not, though, the exclusive preserve of down-at-heel, stoned-out-of-their-brains hippies. Many claim that the source of the most exclusive coffee on Earth is a monkey's backside. Considered the finest coffee in the world during the 19th century, Monkey Coffee gained its unique taste either because the monkeys concerned picked only the best coffee berries or alternatively because of the chemical reaction that occurred as these choice beans passed through the animal's bowels and out. Yes, this was a coffee that was percolated through the digestive system of a monkey. The caffeine-rich monkey droppings were then collected by canny locals and sold to white people who perhaps had more money than sense. Monkey Coffee is still a gourmet product in the USA, where coffee shops sell it for around $15 a cup. The variety on sale today, though, is not actually the product of monkey droppings.

There is, however, a company called The Raven's Brew that retails a coffee called Kopi Luwak under the slogan 'Good to the last dropping'. Raven's Brew claim that their drink's basic ingredient derives from the cleansed droppings of a small nocturnal Indonesian beast called the palm toddy cat. The palm toddy lives on a diet of alcoholic tree sap and coffee beans, and is said to be permanently inebriated, probably very much like some people. It is incapable of digesting the beans, which become imbued with alcohol as they pass through its digestive system. Thus Kopa Luwak coffee gains its unique aroma and flavour.

The tale of this tree-dwelling vegetarian cat with the Latin name *Paradoxurus hermaphroditus* ('paradoxical hermaphrodite') might give a whiff not so much of anally percolated caffeine as of urban legend. The story is, however, true. The toddy is the common palm civet; it is *hermaphroditus* because both male and female toddies have scent glands that resemble testes; and, perhaps most unbelievably of all, there are people in the world willing to shell out $300 a pound for coffee that's been through a small drunk animal's bowels.

Hallucinogenic reindeer juice

Another variation on the idea of drug-infused substances served up direct from the back end of a beast is of course hallucinogenic reindeer urine. According to some authorities, the people of the ancient Samisk tribes, who once inhabited the area now known as Lapland, liked nothing better than to imbibe the urine of reindeer that had eaten Fly Agaric mushrooms.

Fly Agaric is a well-known and highly potent variety of hallucinogenic mushroom. Fresh specimens of this fungus are, however, notoriously poisonous to humans. Supposedly, though, the toxins are removed when the mushrooms are filtered through a reindeer's digestive system. And, luckily, reindeer like eating the mushrooms. To this day they seek out Fly Agarics even when they lie buried under a blanket of snow. So in times past the reindeers would eat the mushrooms and the Samisk shaman would collect the beasts' urine, consume it and enjoy the hallucinogens with which it was imbued.

After drinking the psychedelic reindeer juice, the shaman would enter a trance in which he would fly to a spirit world. Once in this spirit world, he would seek out answers to any problems currently facing the tribe, such as outbreaks of sickness. He would thus return from the spirit world with all the medical knowledge the folks at home wanted.

Think about it. Flying through the air with the reindeer. Coming back to a snowy Lapland scene with that special something everyone has been eagerly waiting for. Re-entering the yurt or tribal dwelling through the chimney which actually happened to double as its entrance. Yes, it is argued that the origin of the tradition of Santa Claus owes much to the Samisk shaman and hallucinogenic mushrooms. Even Santa's red and white outfit is reminiscent of the distinctive colours of the Fly Agaric mushroom.

All this, then, from drinking reindeer urine. Sadly, not quite. This is another story that has undergone a bit of a druggy distortion over time. There is, in fact, little or no evidence of ancient people in Lapland ever drinking reindeer urine. Instead, the tribal shaman would himself have known how to prepare the Fly Agaric mushrooms so they were safe to eat. It is possible that the other people of his tribe then consumed his toxin-free urine in order to enjoy the effects of the mushrooms.

And they might not have been the only ones with a taste for human wee. Even today reindeer will approach human habitations in Scandinavia seeking out a quick snack of yellowy, urine-flavoured snow. It is presumed that the reindeer do this for the benefit of the salts, or urea, that the urine contains. What's more, the reindeer are also known to particularly like urine that contains muscimol, the active chemical in the Fly Agaric.

 ## Scientific results

Macaques may lick out used opium pipes and reindeer may eat snowballs shot with human urine, but one thing that no animal is normally prepared to do is to smoke. Howard Marks in *The Howard Marks Book of Dope Stories* claims that this is the one activity that distinguishes human from animal. Humans smoke. Animals don't. However, animals do smoke when people strap them down in laboratories and force them to, and that is how monkeys came to smoke freebase cocaine. Interestingly, though, after initially smoking freebase because they had been forced to, the monkeys were then prepared, in direct contravention of the Howard Marks rule, to carry on smoking just for their own satisfaction.

Another experiment, in the 1960s, compared the effects of heroin to those of cocaine. One group of rats was given heroin and another was given cocaine. Heroin came out looking positively beneficial to health and happiness. The reason was that although the heroin rats became addicts, the effects of the heroin occasionally made them sleepy. There was therefore a period when they were snoozing and not taking heroin. They even carried on eating, drinking and grooming themselves. In this they showed considerably better sense than many human heroin users.

Cocaine, on the other hand, is a stimulant. The rats who were given cocaine did absolutely nothing except take coke. The only time they stopped was when they collapsed from exhaustion. Sometimes after collapsing they would get up again, in which case they would get straight back to the business of taking more cocaine. Other times, they didn't get up again, because they were dead. And that was the point at which they stopped taking cocaine.

In other tests on cocaine it has always proved to be a substance that animals will carry on taking in favour of anything else, including food, drink and sex. In one experiment chimpanzees were trained to hit a bar in order to be given a shot of cocaine. After they got used to the idea, things were made a little more difficult, to see how just often they would be prepared to hit the bar to get the cocaine. One chimp hit the bar almost 13,000 times to receive a single shot of coke. No wonder coke addicts are such determined, highly driven characters.

At the University of Michigan more chimpanzees were given free access to cocaine and were even taught to inject themselves. The result was much the same as had happened with the rats. The chimps went cocaine crazy. They binged for five days without sleeping. They weren't interested in anything except cocaine. They even stopped interacting in any way with one another. By the end of this chimps' coke party some of the animals had become so agitated that they had gnawed their own fingers off. The experiment was ended because clearly these monkeys were either going to starve themselves to death or choke on their own fingers. This intense cycle of addiction nevertheless ended unexpectedly easily once the injections were taken away. Most of the toxic effects the chimps had suffered were reversed, although some suffered liver damage and none of them grew their fingers back.

DON'T TRY THIS AT HOME ...

In autumn 1884 Carl Koller numbed the cornea of a frog with cocaine solution. He found he could then stick a pin into the frog's eye without causing the creature any distress. So to make sure, he numbed the cornea of his own eye with cocaine, held up a mirror and found he could touch his cornea with a pin. Koller had just discovered cocaine's use as a local anaethestic. Hopefully, no one gave him a congratulatory slap on the back until he'd pulled the pin back out. Also hopefully, he'd given the pin a wipe after taking it out of the frog's eye.

In a third cocaine monkey experiment, the animals were given not the drug cocaine but pellets of the more natural product coca. In this case the monkeys behaved themselves much better. They were offered a coca pellet every five minutes. They could therefore have eaten twelve pellets an hour if they had wished. They didn't. They limited themselves to around one per hour. The cocaine element, though, was still vital for them. When the same experiment was done using pellets that had all the ingredients of coca leaf apart from cocaine, the monkeys were less interested and only ate two or three pellets per day. Video footage of the monkeys showed that they seemed to know instinctively how to take the coca pellets. They chewed and sucked them in more or less the same way that Amerigo Vespucci had described the natives doing when he arrived in South America in the 15th century.

 ## One dog comes clean

So, for whatever reason they become users, animals seem to show a similar level of enthusiasm for drugs as humans. It is therefore reassuring to hear that at least some creatures are prepared to take a more moral stand against such practices.

One dog in Columbus, Ohio, went so far as to take matters into his own paws and phoned the police to turn in his drug-abusing owner. In fact, what he did was accidentally press the speed dial for 911 on his owner's mobile while they were out driving around together. At the other end of the line police presumed that the sounds of doggy yelps and panting they heard were the sobs of a distraught woman. So they traced the call, sped round to the house of the owner of the mobile phone and smashed their way in. There, of course, they found no emergency but they did find 150 healthy but illegal marijuana plants growing in the basement. Master was arrested on his return. Presumably there was no choccy treat for Fido that night.

ARTISTIC VISIONS

 ## Artistic excess

The writer Pete McCarthy once made an observation of great insight. Why, he asked, had so many great artists throughout history – whether painters, poets, writers or musicians – been so predisposed to alcoholic excess? Was it because of their great artistic sensitivity? Was it to quell the demons raging

 'IF you don't believe drugs have done great things for us, go home tonight and take all your albums, all your tapes and all your CDs and burn them. Because you know what? The musicians who made all that great music that's enhanced your lives throughout the years were all real high on drugs.'

– Bill Hicks

inside them? Was it because they were seeking inspiration? No. The explanation was far simpler. It was because, unlike the rest of us, they didn't have to get up and go out to work in the morning. This pearl of wisdom might equally be applied to drug-taking, which has been another popular leisure pursuit among the artistic fraternity. Spare time plus boredom equals indulgence. And creative types – in company with the rich, the famous and the unemployed – tend to have lots of spare time.

 ## Impossible Romantics

At the turn of the 19th century, the Romantic movement in poetry had brought about a revolution in literature. Samuel Taylor Coleridge and William Wordsworth were the movement's initial leading exponents. Coleridge was also a notorious opium addict. He insisted that he had been 'seduced' into his drug habit after opium had been prescribed for swollen knees and indigestion thanks to 'a most unhappy Quackery'. Wordsworth's sister, Dorothy, identified Coleridge as 'the slave of stimulants'. Like many a junkie after him, Coleridge's 'whole time and thoughts' were, according to Dorothy, 'employed in deceiving himself, and seeking to deceive others' except for 'when he was reading'.

At the time Coleridge wrote his poem 'Kubla Khan', he was known to be taking opium for dysentery and perhaps for the stress caused by financial worries. The story goes that while staying at a farmhouse on Exmoor he fell asleep as a result of having taken 'an anodyne' halfway through reading a work about Kubla Khan and his stately palace at Xanadu. Three hours later, when he woke up, Coleridge realised he had just come up with a 300-line poem in his sleep. He began to write down his opium-inspired visions of Kubla Khan's 'caverns measureless to man', the 'sunny pleasure-dome' and the 'caves of ice'. When he reached line 54 there was a knock at the door. Coleridge was, as he put it in his introduction to the poem, 'unfortunately called out by a person on business from Porlock, and detained by him above an hour'. When he got back to the writing desk he found he was unable to remember another word of his poem. That's drugs for you.

Of the other Romantic poets, Lord Byron was also an occasional user of laudanum, although in 1821 he wrote that he didn't 'like laudanum now as I used to do'. Shelley seems to have been a heavier user, while Keats took laudanum in 1819 and 1820 and intended to kill himself by means of the drug. Keats died before he could carry out his intention. The novelist Sir Walter Scott was also a significant user, taking 200 drops of laudanum plus six grains of opium a day around the time he was writing *The Bride of Lammermoor*.

 ## True confessions

Another occasional house guest of the Wordsworths at Grasmere was an even more notorious opium user than Coleridge. In the early 1800s the teenage Thomas De Quincey was living in near starvation in London. Despite his penury, he was in the habit of washing his head with cold water each day.

When, one day in 1804, he developed toothache, he presumed this was because he hadn't washed his head that day. After giving his head a really good wash in some very cold water indeed, he went to bed with cold, wet hair. He awoke the next day in excruciating pain which persisted for weeks, until one wet, cheerless Sunday afternoon he bought opium, for the first time in his life, from a druggist near the Parthenon in Oxford Street. The opium seemed to do slightly more than relieve De Quincey's neuralgia:

> I took it:—and in an hour, oh! heavens! ... What an upheaving, from its lowest depths, of the inner spirits! ... Here was a panacea ... for all human woes; here was the secret of happiness, about which philosophers had disputed for so many ages ... happiness might now be bought for a penny, and carried in the waistcoat pocket.

De Quincey went on to use opium specifically for pleasure. More than 150 years before the practice of taking drugs to enjoy rock concerts began, De Quincy was setting aside one evening a week to go out and enjoy concerts and operas while under the influence of opium. According to Richard Davenport-Hines in *The Pursuit of Oblivion* 'these musical opium evenings established De Quincey as among the first Europeans consciously to take a drug to enhance aesthetic pleasure rather than to desensitise pain'. By 1815 De Quincey was on 329 grains of opium or 8,000 drops of laudanum a day. A few years later this was up to 480 grains of opium.

In 1821, still beset by financial problems, De Quincey began to write the work which made him famous, *The Confessions of an English Opium Eater*. The *Confessions* appeared in the *London Magazine* and was an immediate success. The use of 'confessions' as a book title was novel, although since De Quincey it has been used very frequently for its suggestion of religious redemption and the titillating details of sordid depravity that will feature along the way.

Despite occasional attempts at abstinence, De Quincey carried on using opium until his death in December 1859 at the age of 74. He had also experimented with other drugs. In later life he mentioned in an eassy that he had 'tried everything in this world except "bang", which I believe is obtained from hemp'. A reader remedied this deficiency and supplied De Quincey with some 'bang', or hashish, soon afterwards.

De Quincey's *Confessions*, like many other such later works, seems to have led enthusiastic readers into drug use themselves. Following its publication, a doctor claimed to know of several cases in which patients had died or had nearly killed themselves by taking opium after reading this work which was 'of universal ill tendency'. One youth who began taking opium in imitation of De Quincey was Branwell Brontë, the doomed artist brother of Charlotte, Emily and Anne.

Charles Dickens began to take opium towards the end of his life. He was driven to drugs for the same reason that led a lot of later artists to develop a habit. He was on tour in America. Physically drained by his dramatic readings from his novels, Dickens kept himself going with drugs.

Dickens's friend, the novelist Wilkie Collins, seems to

have been almost as enthusiastic about opium as De Quincey had been. 'Who was the man who invented laudanum?' demanded Collins. 'I thank him from the bottom of my heart.' Collins carried a silver flask of laudanum with him everywhere he went, kept a decanter of laudanum at home and drank a wine glass full each night before bed. His 1868 novel, *The Moonstone*, was dictated entirely under the influence of opium and concerns, perhaps inevitably, an insomniac who has been prescribed opium and also an opium addict. The poet Elizabeth Barrett Browning was, on the other hand, described as 'a well-balanced addict'. Her husband, Robert Browning, was surprised to find that sleep only came to her 'in a red hood of poppies'.

In 1895 Oscar Wilde wrote of his visit to Algiers with Lord Alfred Douglas, 'Bosie and I have taken to haschish: it is quite exquisite: three puffs of smoke and then peace and love.' The 'peace and love' to which Oscar wittily alludes refers in fact to sex with young boys. Victor Hugo was another hashish user, as was Edgar Allan Poe and the Irish poet W.B.Yeats, who experimented with it with his lover, Maud Gonne, in an attempt to develop telepathic powers. This led, apparently, to limited success, with Gonne finding herself transported to the bedside of her sister.

 ## Dr Jekyll and Mr Hyde

In Robert Louis Stevenson's classic tale, respectable Dr Jekyll takes a chemical potion and undergoes a terrifying transformation which unleashes his monstrous alter ego, Mr Hyde.

Some allege that in this work Robert Louis Stevenson portrayed the effects of taking cocaine. As Dr Jekyll first takes his compound drug he describes its effects:

I came to myself as if out of a great sickness. There was something strange in my sensations, something indescribably new and, from its very novelty, incredibly sweet. I felt younger, lighter, happier in body; within I was conscious of a heady recklessness, a current of disordered sensual images running like a mill race in my fancy, a solution of the bonds of obligation, an unknown but not an innocent freedom of the soul.

Some suggest that the influence of cocaine on the work may go further. In October 1885 Stevenson completed a 60,000 word draft of *Dr Jekyll and Mr Hyde* in six days. This would be remarkable going for anyone, but Stevenson was supposedly a bedridden invalid. Mrs Stevenson, however, routinely studied the medical journal the *Lancet* in search of possible cures for her husband. And in 1885 the *Lancet* was full of testimonials detailing the effects of the new miracle drug, cocaine.

Others claim that Stevenson was using laudanum, but perhaps coke would seem the more energising compound. So could Stevenson's genius on this occasion have been a case of 99 per cent perspiration and 1 per cent inhalation?

CLASSIC DRUG READS – NON-FICTION

Confessions of an English Opium Eater, **Thomas De Quincey:** Opium addiction in the early 19th century by the friend of Coleridge and Wordsworth.

Opium, **Jean Cocteau:** Cocteau's description of his descent into life as a drug addict in the 1920s following the death of his protégé, Raymond Radiguet.

Junky, **William S. Burroughs:** Straightforwardly titled, Burroughs's first book, published in 1953 under the pseudonym William Lee, is a deadpan account of his junkie life.

The Doors of Perception, **Aldous Huxley:** A celebration and investigation of mescaline, the substance that Huxley believed could, in William Blake's words, cleanse the doors of perception so that 'everything would appear to man as it is, infinite'. Published in 1954, the book was an inspiration to Jim Morrison and friends 10 years or so later.

The Yage Letters, **William S. Burroughs and Allen Ginsberg:** Burroughs's 1953 exploration of Ecuador and Peru in search of yage or ayahuasca or, as he puts it, the 'final fix' preserved in a literary exchange with his fellow Beat, Ginsberg.

The Electric Kool-Aid Acid Test, **Tom Wolfe:** Life on the road with Ken Kesey, Neal Cassady and the Merry Pranksters as they evangelically spread the word about LSD to the good people of early 1960s America.

Guilty of Everything, **Herbert Huncke:** Autobiography of Huncke – a hustler in the 1930s and 40s, friend of the Beats after World War Two and the man who turned William Burroughs on to heroin. Huncke was depicted not only by Burroughs in *Junkie* but also by Ginsberg in his poem 'Howl' and by Kerouac in the character of Elmo Hassel in *On the Road*. According to Kerouac, 'the greatest storyteller I know'.

***Mr Nice*, Howard Marks:** Highly readable, bestselling autobiography from the most popular Oxford-educated, ex-secret service employee, drug dealer and money launderer to have come out of Wales.

***Snowblind*, Robert Sabbag:** Sabbag's classic tale of Zachary Swan, a legendary cocaine smuggler of the 1960s and 70s who runs rings around police and customs officials with his scams.

***Smokescreen*, Robert Sabbag:** The life story of Allen Long, America's Mr Nice, the man who upped the quantity and quality of US marijuana for several years in the 1970s. Long was a documentary film-maker, pilot and dope connoisseur who risked everything for the Beluga caviar of marijuana, Columbian Santa Marta Gold. Long moved into smuggling to fund one of his projects and sought out Sabbag to author his story set against the good old days of drugs trafficking before the cartels got involved.

***Prozac Nation*, Elizabeth Wurtzel:** Beginning as a schoolgirl carving her calves with a razor to a backdrop of Velvet Underground tunes, Wurtzel goes on to a life in which full-blown depression hits her not as a 'sudden disaster' but like 'accumulated data'. She gets into speed and ecstasy and finally attempts suicide. Although redeemed finally by Prozac, which she sees as both a national joke and a life saver, in her subsequent work, *More, Now, Again*, Wurtzel has become a Ritalin user and is again setting about her legs, this time with a pair of tweezers, until they are a mottle of sores and abcesses.

CLASSIC DRUG READS – FICTION

Under the Volcano, **Malcolm Lowry:** Geoffrey Firmin, British consul in Mexico, depicted in his last few hours as he finally destroys himself on the hallucinogenic local brew, mescal.

The Man With the Golden Arm, **Nelson Algren:** The tale of Frankie Machine, ex-soldier and morphine addict, famously filmed with Frank Sinatra and Kim Novak, written by the man who shared the affections of Simone de Beauvoir with Jean-Paul Sartre.

Island, **Aldous Huxley:** Huxley's final novel, set in Pala – a fictional utopian commune based around hallucinogens, sexual freedom and Eastern religion – as it is visited by Will Farnaby, a journalist interested in the culture but whose boss owns a large petroleum company.

Fear and Loathing in Las Vegas, **Hunter S. Thompson:** Thompson's fantastical 1971 account of heavily drug-fuelled attendance at a political convention in company with Oscar Zeta Acosta, 567-kilogram (1,250-pound) Chicago attorney.

Less Than Zero, **Brett Easton Ellis:** Sex and drugs lifestyle of a degenerate but highly affluent group of young Los Angelinos in the 1980s; as the central character Clay drives aimlessly about the city in a reflection of the lack of inner direction brought on by knowing and owning everything.

Bright Lights, Big City, **Jay McInerney:** McInerney's first novel. 'Bolivian marching powder' snorting highly successful 20-something American comes to realise he has nothing. McInerney explored a similar theme from a female perspective in his subsequent work, *Story of My Life.*

Cain's Book, **Alexander Trocchi:** Celebrated novel of the 1960s based on the addicted experiences of its Scottish-Italian author. Earlier in his life Trocchi had been a Paris left-bank guru to the likes of Terry Southern but was reduced to writing pornography to fund his drug habit. Although he lived for another 24 years, *Cain's Book* was Trocchi's last published work.

The Basketball Diaries, **Jim Carroll:** Carroll's first book, based on his personal experiences between the ages of 12 and 16 'growing up hip' as a rising basketball star who had won a scholarship to a prestigious Catholic school but who fell into a world of stealing, hustling gay men and heroin addiction. Later made into a film starring Leonardo di Caprio.

Novel With Cocaine, **M. Ageyev:** The tale of Vadim Maslennikov, a young Russian hedonist living at the time of the Russian revolution, who descends into a life of drug abuse, liaisons with prostitutes and self-hatred. The book was published pseudonymously in the early 1930s, and the real identity of the author has never been established. *Novel With Cocaine* was the book found at the bedside of Manic Street Preacher Richey Edwards on the day he disappeared. There's a recommendation for you.

Postcards From the Edge, **Carrie Fisher:** The one-time *Stars Wars* star's witty semi-autobiographical tales of a young actress struggling out of drug re-hab and her overbearing mum.

Trainspotting, **Irvine Welsh:** An instant hit, this is the story of the sometimes hilarious but disturbingly realistic interwoven lives of a group of no-hope smack addicts in 1990s Edinburgh. It is unclear

Twentieth-century writers

In the 20th century the poet W.H. Auden began to use Benzedrine on a daily basis to get his mind up and running ready for the business of poetry. Aldous Huxley celebrated his hallucinogenic experiences on mescaline and LSD in his books *The Doors of Perception* and *Heaven and Hell.* Huxley believed that the brain filtered daily experience but hallucinogenic drugs were capable of opening the doors of perception. On his deathbed in 1963, Huxley asked to be given LSD so he could die under its effects. The psychiatrist who helped administer Huxley's drugs was Humphrey Osmond, who, in

whether Welsh's vivid descriptions of heroin use are based on personal experience but other users confirm that he seems to know his subject extraordinarily well. Recently he has returned to the characters of *Trainspotting* in his book *Porno.*

***Cocaine Nights*, J.G. Ballard:** On the Costa del Sol, Frank Prentice is imprisoned after he has confessed to a horrific act of arson of which he is clearly innocent. His brother Charles begins to investigate the ugly truth about the once sleepy retirement haven in which Frank lived, whose ageing inhabitants have recently been buzzing with a peculiar new-found energy.

***Go Now*, Richard Hell:** A profoundly honest account of the trials and tribulations of kicking a heroin habit in this 1996 novel from former Television and Voidoid guitarist. It tells the tale of Billy Mud, a punk musician and addict, on the road from LA to New York.

'THE remarkable thing is that I stupefied myself from 1948 to 1963. A long time – that's 15 years pre-occupied with one thought.'

– Allen Ginsberg

1957, came up with the term 'psychedelic' to describe the effects of hallucinogens.

The 1950s Beat writers Jack Kerouac, Allen Ginsberg and William Burroughs had met while at Columbia University in New York in the 1940s. Ginsberg dedicated his life to a systematic exploration of the mind and used heroin, mescaline, peyote and psilocybin to assist in the quest. In London, Ginsberg thanked Dame Edith Sitwell for having championed his work by offering the 71-year-old poet a dose of heroin. Dame Edith wasn't entirely impressed as the heroin brought her out in spots.

Ginsberg was turned on to hallucinogens in the form of psilocybin by his friend Timothy Leary in the early 1960s. Ginsberg's reaction was to strip naked in Leary's house and wander around saying, 'I'm the Messiah. I've come to preach love to the world. We're going to walk through the streets and teach people to love.' Ginsberg had just instantaneously summed up the entire hippy movement of the next 10 years.

Similarly, Burroughs was a heroin user from 1945. During this time he went to Mexico, wrote his novel *Junky* and killed his wife along the way. Mrs Burroughs was in fact shot during a game of William Tell in which hubby used a gun instead of a bow and arrow and balanced a glass on her head in place of the apple. Luckily, the police believed Burroughs's story that it was an accident and no charges were brought.

Burroughs carried on using heroin and other drugs until a Dr Dent helped him kick his habit. Burroughs made sure Dr Dent got a credit in every book he went on to write until his death in 1997, at the age of 83. Unfortunately, his son, William Burroughs Junior, did not seek the services of Dr Dent and died 16 years before his father of drug and alcohol addiction.

Slightly younger than the Beats was Ken Kesey who, in 1959, volunteered for experiments into the effects of hallucinogens being run at Menlo Park Veterans Administration Hospital. Kesey also got a job at the hospital as a janitor on the psychiatric ward. While doing a night shift under the effects of mescaline, Kesey had a vision of a mute schizophrenic Native American. This figure was to become the narrator of his great novel *One Flew Over the Cuckoo's Nest* published in 1962.

Two years later, following the success of his second novel *Sometimes a Great Notion*, Kesey acquired a 1939 International Harvester bus, decorated it with swirls of psychedelic colour and assembled a group of proto-hippies known as the Merry Pranksters. Putting literature aside, Kesey's mission was now actively to share the revelation he had found in LSD with the world. So with Neal Cassady – Beat contemporary of Burroughs et al. and the model for Kerouac's Dean Moriarty in *On the Road* – at the wheel, Kesey's Pranksters set off across the United States in June 1964. At each stopping point the locals were provided with samples of a concoction known as Kool Aid. Kesey's Kool

IT'S SIMPLY NOT REAL, MAN

The top fictional drugs dreamt up for classic works of literature:

Soma In *Brave New World*, Aldous Huxley's 1932 vision of the future, Soma is a Prozac-like drug used to instil a constant state of 'perfect pleasure'. Soma provides the user with the sense of a 'warm ... richly coloured ... infinitely friendly world' and has 'all the advantages of Christianity and alcohol' but 'none of their defects'. Indeed it is taken in a sacramental manner:

> The service had begun. The dedicated soma tablets were placed in the centre of the table. The loving cup of strawberry ice-cream soma was passed from hand to hand and, with the formula, 'I drink to my annihilation', 12 times quaffed.

Vurt Jeff Noon's novel *Vurt* tells of the search of Scribble for his sister Desdemona in a bleak, industrial, futuristic Manchester peopled by robo-men, dog-men, shadow women and zombies. The world Desdemona has been lost to is only accessible through a psychedelic drug known as vurt, taken by tickling the back of the throat with a yellow feather. Noon's subsequent book, *Pollen*, developed the idea of a drug that enabled its users to step into their own dreams.

Can-D and Chew-Z Philip K. Dick's work *The Three Stigmata of Palmer Eldritch* begins with the inhabitants of Earth exiled to a miserable existence on Mars, where their only relief is a chewing gum-based drug called Can-D. When a figure called Palmer Eldritch arrives from a distant galaxy he brings a new drug, Chew-Z, capable of taking its users into a new illusory world of immortality and wish fulfilment. The catch is that Eldritch enters and acts as God in the Chew-Z users' private universes. Dick notoriously wrote much of his fiction under the influence of amphetamines.

Spiked moloko Anthony Burgess's 1962 novel *A Clockwork Orange* is a nightmare vision of a violent futuristic youth culture. The book focuses on Alex and his droogs and their addiction to drugs such as drencrom, synthemesc (the effects of which sound like a cross between acid and heroin) and vellocet (a sort of violence-inducing speed), which they drink mixed with milk or moloko served from the teat of female mannequins at the Korova milkbar. The result of synthemesc, as Alex observes, can be that 'you got the messel that everything all round you was sort of in the past ... And you were sort of hypnotised by your boot or shoe or a finger-nail' until eventually 'the lights started cracking like atomics and the boot or finger-nail ... turned into a big big big mesto, bigger than the whole world and you were just going to get introduced to old Bog or God ...'

Dylar In Don Delillo's *White Noise* Jack is a lecturer in Hitler studies at College-on-the-Hill and, after several divorces, is currently married to Babette. Following a secret trial, Babette has become addicted to Dylar, an unlicensed drug that overcomes fear of death and causes individuals to mistake words for the objects to which they refer. As Dylar has been withdrawn for being too dangerous, Babette now has to obtain her supplies in return for sex in a motel room with the trial organiser.

CLASSIC DRUGS MOVIES OF THE 20TH CENTURY

A Squeedunk Sherlock Holmes (1909) Early silent film burlesque based on the famous detective which included the first depiction of cocaine use on film.

The Mystery of the Leaping Fish (1916) A silent comedy caper starring Douglas Fairbanks Senior as Inspector Coke Ennyday on the trail of a criminal mastermind. Along the way Inspector Coke is explicitly shown consuming and injecting copious amounts of cocaine and opium and even using them to overpower the baddies.

The Pace That Kills (1930) A cautionary tale about the slide into drug addiction and the inevitable criminality, prostitution, family break-up and death that go with it.

Marijuana (1935) A nice girl gets involved with marijuana. The result: nudity and illegitimate children.

Reefer Madness (1936) Another cautionary tale, this time about high school kids Jimmy, Bill and pals who get hooked on marijuana by evil dealers Mae and Ralph. Shocking scenes of lewdness, insanity, murder and crazed piano-playing soon follow.

Cocaine Fiends (1936) A nice young girl in the big city is turned into a coke addict by a dope-peddling mobster. You know what happens next. Essentially a remake of *The Pace That Kills*.

Assassin of Youth (1937) An old lady killed by marijuana-crazed youths leaves her inheritance to her granddaughter, Joan, on condition that she lead a clean life. Joan's cousin Linda gets her involved with marijuana to ruin her reputation. Insanity and attempted murder follow.

The Man With the Golden Arm (1955) Otto Preminger's film of Nelson Algren's novel starring Frank Sinatra as Frankie Machine, the drug addict/jazz musician/card dealer and his attempts to go straight. Caused a sensation because the drugged-up hero shown in the film was a white man.

Monkey On My Back (1957) A frank portrayal of destructive addiction based on the true story of a boxer who became addicted to morphine while serving at Guadalcanal.

Paris Blues (1961) Paul Newman as a jazz musician trying to cure his friend of cocaine addiction.

Valley of the Dolls (1967) Sharon Tate, Patty Duke, Barbara Parkins and Susan Hayward in an exploration of the sufferings of three ambitious women trying to break into the world of show business and their reliance on 'dolls', or pills.

Easy Rider (1969) Peter Fonda and Dennis Hopper cross the United States carrying a load of cocaine that they intend to sell to record producer Phil Spector. Spector's real-life Christmas card that year featured a picture of himself snorting a line and captioned, 'A little snow at Christmas never hurt anyone'.

Superfly (1972) A blaxploitation classic about a cocaine dealer in Harlem who has to eliminate the syndicate kingpins keeping him down in order to get out of the business.

Drugstore Cowboy (1989) Gus Van Sant's film about a group of desperate addicts on the run from the police, robbing pharmacies en route. Features a cameo appearance by junkie legend William Burroughs.

Pulp Fiction (1994) Tarantino's movie was criticised at the time of its release for glamorising drug abuse so much that it may have encouraged heroin injection. The director was quoted as saying he wanted to direct 'the best shooting-up scene in the world' and John Travolta stabbing a syringe of adrenalin direct into Uma Thurman's heart must be pretty hard to beat.

Trainspotting (1996) Classic adaptation of Irvine Welsh's tales of addicted Edinburgh folk, featuring Ewan MacGregor being subsumed into one of the most disgusting toilet bowls ever seen.

Christiana F (1981) German film about an intravenous heroin abuser which was praised, in contrast to *Pulp Fiction* and *Trainspotting*, for showing the wretchedness of life on smack. Unfortunately, it did this in such an uncompromising manner that audiences found it far too depressing and the film was not a box office success.

Aid recipe was fairly straightforward. First take some orange juice. Then put some LSD in it. One dollar bought as much Kool Aid as you could drink. Kesey's acid tests continued on the road and back at his base in La Honda, San Francisco, where local group The Warlocks – later to change their name to The Grateful Dead – provided accompaniment for the proceedings.

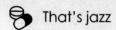

That's jazz

In the world of 20th-century popular music, New Orleans jazz is said to have been built on bourbon, 1930s swing on marijuana and 1940s and 50s bebop on heroin. Louis Armstrong was said to have been an enthusiastic 'viper', or marijuana user, from the time he returned to Chicago from New York in 1925. Armstrong admitted using marijuana virtually every day, describing it as 'an assistant, a friend, a nice cheap drink'. To him it seemed safer than alcohol and was similar to the natural herbs and grasses with which his mother had fed and cured him as a boy.

During the 1930s there were often explicit references to cannabis and cocaine in the lyrics and even the titles of popular songs. Harry 'the Hipster' Gibson and Cab Calloway both specialised in novelty tunes which used the latest inner-city drugs slang for the delectation of mainstream white audiences. Cab Calloway featured in Hollywood cinema productions celebrating, for example, figures such as 'the Reefer Man'. Gibson had a major hit in 1944 with the splendidly titled *Who Put the Benzedrine in Mrs Murphy's Ovaltine?*. The cheerful-sounding Harry the Hipster was not, however, named without due reason. Although he found fame as a popular recording artist, Gibson had sensibly developed a day job to fall back on. Unfortunately, this day job was working as a heroin dealer. As such he supplied fellow artistes such as singer Anita O'Day.

TOP EXPLICIT DRUGS TUNES FROM THE 1920s TO 40s

'A Viper's Moan', Willie Bryant and His Orchestra (1935)

'Blue Reefer Blues', Richard M. Jones and His Jazz Wizards (1935)

'Cocaine', Dick Justice

'Cocaine Blues', Luke Jordan (1927)

'Cocaine Habit Blues', The Memphis Jug Band (1930)

'Dope Head Blues', Victoria Spivey and Lonnie Johnson (1927)

'If You're a Viper', Bob Howard and His Boys (1938)

'Jerry the Junker', Clarence Williams and His Washboard Band (1934)

'Junker's Blues', Champion Jack Dupree (1940)

'Lotus Blossom (Sweet Marijuana)', Julia Lee and Her Boy Friends (1947)

'Ol' Man River (Smoke a Little Tea)', Cootie Williams and His Rug Cutters (1938)

'Pipe Dream Blues', Hazel Meyers

'Reefer Head Woman', Jazz Gillum and His Jazz Boys (1938)

'Reefer Hound Blues', Curtis Jones (1938)

'Reefer Man', Baron Lee and the Blue Rhythm Band (1932)

'Reefer Man', Don Redman and His Orchestra (1932)

'Reefer Song', Fats Waller (1943)

'Save the Roach for Me', Buck Washington (1944)

'Smoking Reefers', Larry Adler (1938)

'Sweet Marijuana Brown', Barney Biggard Sextet (1945)

'Take a Whiff on Me', Leadbelly (1934)

'The Reefer Song', Fats Waller (1943)

'The Stuff Is Here and It's Mellow', Cleo Brown (1935)

'The Weed Smoker's Dream (Why Don't You Do Right?)', The Harlem Hamfats (1936)

'Viper Mad', Sidney Bechet with Noble Sissle's Swingsters (1938)

'Wackey Dust', Chick Webb and His Orchestra with Ella Fitzgerald (1938)

'When I Get Low, I Get High', Chick Webb and His Orchestra with Ella Fitzgerald (1936)

Bebop

While Louis Armstrong was an enthusiastic weed smoker, even sharing joints with Bing Crosby, he knew that the favoured drug of the next jazz generation was different. Armstrong called heroin 'drastic stuff'. As Artie Shaw noted, 'Jazz was born in a whiskey barrel, grew up on marijuana and is about to expire on heroin.'

Heroin had become known as a form of solace for the hard lives endured by some black people in the first half of the 20th century. Bebop jazz seemed to express a sense of isolation and detachment from the world akin to the effects of heroin. The leading exponent of the bebop movement was Charlie Parker, who seemed to be in a hermetically sealed world of his own when he played. There was a good reason for this. 'This is my home,' he told a friend as he rolled up his sleeve to inject himself.

Parker's appetite for drugs was legendary. On one occasion pianist Hampton Hawes described how he watched in disbelief as Parker chain-smoked marijuana, downed eleven shots of whisky with a handful of Benzedrine capsules and then, obviously for a bit of a chaser, shot up with heroin. Parker then 'sweated like a horse for five minutes', got up, put his suit on and 'half an hour later was on the stand playing strong and beautiful'.

'YOU can get it out of your body, but you can't get it out of your brain.'
– Charlie Parker

Parker once even signed all his royalties over to his dealer, while the first notes of his tune 'Mood' were used as a signal by users wanting to attract their dealer's attention. When Charlie Parker died in March 1955, the coroner estimated him to have been around 55 to 60 years old. This is indeed what pictures of him in his later years would suggest. In fact Charlie Parker was 34 years old when he died.

 ## The influence of heroin

Among aspiring jazz musicians of the 1940s and 50s the idea began to circulate that if you wanted to play saxophone like Charlie Parker, you had to take heroin like Charlie Parker. This idea did seem to be borne out by one obvious fact. Charlie Parker himself was only able to play the way he did after taking the drug. The reason for this was not, however, that heroin was a magic potion capable of inducing spectacular jazz ability in those who took it. The reason was that Charlie Parker was a heroin addict. He needed to take heroin to be able to do anything. And that included playing the saxophone.

Other jazz musicians seem to have had equally huge appetites for drugs. By 1961 a survey showed that 16 per cent of the jazz musicians in New York were drug addicts and more still were regular users. If heroin wasn't always taken just out of hero worship it was certainly regarded as a working drug. No matter what shape you were in, a shot of heroin would always get you fit to play on stage.

The index of saxophonist Art Pepper's autobiography

gives an idea of the lifestyle some jazz musicians were pursuing. Under the heading 'drugs', separate entries are listed for 'acid', 'amyl nitrite', 'cocaine', 'cough mixture', 'glue-sniffing', 'marijuana', 'nutmeg' and 'various pills'. Alcoholism, methadone, dolophine and various other substances appear elsewhere in the index, and there is also a heading 'prisons', as a result of the heists, robberies, burglaries and armed assaults that Pepper was involved in between jazz sessions.

Billie Holiday helpfully pointed out the fallacy in the idea of drugs as a means to create great art. 'If you think you need stuff to play music or sing, you're crazy,' she said. 'It can fix you so you can't play nothing or sing nothing.' Billie Holiday, though, had her own addiction problems. Fellow jazz singer Anita O'Day described how she would inject her feet with 10 cc of dissolved heroin to avoid track marks appearing on her arms. When she ran out of veins on the rest of her body, she took to injecting into the side of her vagina. While she was recovering after collapsing in a coma in 1959, the police raided Holiday's hospital room and found a small amount of heroin. She died aged 45 with armed police guarding her hospital room door, in case she decided to commit any more criminal acts.

A ridiculously brief history of drugs in rock and roll

In the world of country music not only did the truckers who listened to Hank Williams keep themselves going on speed

'MAN, The Beatles were so high they even let Ringo sing on a couple of tunes.'

– Bill Hicks

tablets, so did Williams himself. The 29-year-old Williams's intake of alcohol and amphetamines led to a fatal heart attack on New Year's Eve 1953. Following performances, truckers would tip Jerry Lee Lewis with Benzedrine tablets. The young Elvis Presley also got involved in amphetamines. Presley didn't get started on speed as a result of his contacts in the music industry, however. It was his sergeant in the army after his call-up who gave him pills to help keep him awake on guard duty.

The history of rock and roll since the 1950s seems to have been coloured by every type of drug in turn. John Lennon spoke of how periods in The Beatles' recording career could be classified according to the drugs they were taking at the time. Their early rock and roll energy came from the Preludin pills they took in Hamburg; by the time of *Rubber Soul's* mellower acoustic sounds in 1965 the influence was more from marijuana; the loftier and more colourful visions of *Sergeant Pepper* were attributed to LSD, while the stark desperation of tunes like 'I'm So Tired' on *The White Album* came courtesy of Lennon's heroin intake.

The 1970s brought amphetamine energy back to the fore with punk rock as well as bands like the noticeably speed-charged Motörhead. Motörhead bassist Lemmy noted how his system seemed particularly to have adapted to the drug.

By 1979 Sid Vicious was dead of a heroin overdose, while rock music marched on to the cocaine-charged bravado and excess of the late 1970s and 80s. During this period it is alleged that at a party held by the rock group Queen a dwarf was employed to offer party-goers cocaine from a large silver bowl. During the same period *Melody Maker* journalist Chris Maund pointed out, 'If most of those groups at Live Aid had donated their cocaine bills for the year, it would have saved as many lives.' The 1980s and 90s saw ecstasy's rise as a dance floor favourite incorporating many of the qualities of the amphetamines and hallucinogens that had gone before it.

Rock has continued to embody all manner of substance abuse in the most public manner. Revelations that rock stars take drugs are simply no longer news. In the 1990s Noel Gallagher of Oasis managed to stir up controversy by claiming that taking drugs was 'like having a cup of tea in the morning'. As ever, it is debatable whether famous musicians encourage drug use by their comments and actions or just give a public face to what the rest of their generation is up to anyway. If rock stars are advertising agents for drug dealers then they are, of course, not solely to blame.

In 1967 Paul McCartney gave the honest answer 'yes' when an interviewer asked him whether he had ever taken

'BOB Dylan thought the line "I can't hide" was "I get high", so he came with some really good grass ... How could you not dig a bloke like that? He thought we were used to drugs.'

– John Lennon

LSD, but added, 'I'll tell you what. I'll keep quiet about this if you will.' And, indeed, many of today's stars in the worlds of music, television, sports and film do keep very quiet about their drug habits.

 ## Sneaky references

Back in the 1960s our national moral guardians decided that drugged-up musicians liked nothing better than to slip endless references to their chemical habits into their songs. So, for example, some authorities argued in all seriousness that 'Yellow Submarine' by The Beatles is not a song about a man who sailed to sea in a yellow submarine as might at first be thought. Rather it is a song about taking Nembutal, a yellow-coloured downer. 'The Candy Man', as performed by Sammy Davis Junior, has similarly been accused of referring to Nembutal and amphetamines, while 'Walk Like An Egyptian' by The Bangles is, apparently, about smoking marijuana. 'Bridge Over Troubled Water' by Simon and Garfunkel is a surreptitious ode to the joys of heroin, as is The Beatles' 'Hey Jude'. Jude is, of course, short for Judas Iscariot, the friend who is out to betray you, while the song's lyrics clearly state, 'The minute you let it under your skin, then you begin to make it better ...' Well, no they don't. The lyrics are in fact, 'The minute you let *her* under your skin ...' Perhaps even more pertinently, the song's principal writer, Paul McCartney, has admitted to taking LSD, taking and getting over cocaine (around 1966, before anyone else had started taking it) and taking cannabis. Just to make this last admission a little more strongly, Paul has even gone so far as to get himself caught both carrying cannabis through customs and also growing it in his back garden. The admirably honest McCartney does not seem ever to have been associated with heroin.

'Hey Jude' actually began as McCartney's song for John Lennon's son Julian at the time of his parents' marriage break-up. An early version of the lyrics was 'Hey Jules'. A year or so before he inadvertently instigated the 'Hey Jude' ruckus, the four-year-old Julian Lennon was behind another scandalous drugs reference in a popular song. John Lennon always insisted that one day Julian had brought home a painting that showed a girl from his school called Lucy in the sky with diamonds. Moral guardians were quick to spot that the initials of the acid-tinged tune that resulted were LITSWD and that these included the letters LSD.

Roger McGuinn similarly insists to this day that, despite his 1960s drug intake, his song 'Eight Miles High' is about an aeroplane. It owes its title to a miscalculation of the height attained by a plane on which The Byrds were travelling.

It has seriously been claimed that the phrase 'It's fun to smoke marijuana' can just about be heard if the Queen song 'Another One Bites the Dust' is played backwards. People making this claim clearly missed a very obvious point. If Freddie Mercury, the man who publicised one of his records by filling a racing track with naked girls on bicycles, had wanted to encourage people to smoke marijuana, he wouldn't have done it in a shy way.

If a decent rock musician wanted to write a song about,

say, heroin, then he would probably just call the tune 'Heroin'. Lou Reed's song 'Heroin' was recorded originally by The Velvet Underground. Rather than being a furtive attempt to lure the unwary into drug abuse, Reed's song is, of course, an unflinchingly honest piece of art about the highs and lows of its subject matter. Lou made another obvious point about such works that both moral guardians and fans should take on board: 'Just because I write about it, doesn't mean that I do it.'

'Puff the Magic Dragon' by Peter, Paul and Mary, on the other hand, is definitely about marijuana smoking. And, of course, about transvestism as well. Drag-on – geddit?

The stupid club

Rock and roll, perhaps more than other art forms, has also given us the phenomenon of the celebrity overdose – or at least the death in which drugs are implicated. When Kurt Cobain shot himself in 1994, forensic examination revealed that he had heroin in his bloodstream. Kurt's mother made a

CLASSIC ROCK AND ROLL DEATHS

Brian Jones (age 27), 3 July 1969

Jimi Hendrix (age 27), 18 September 1970

Janis Joplin (age 27), 4 October 1970

Jim Morrison, (age 27), 3 July 1971

simple but insightful comment on the tragedy: 'Now he's gone and joined that stupid club. I told him not to join that stupid club.' Mrs Cobain's stupid club of dead rock stars was perhaps founded by the cluster of rock deaths between 1969 and 1971.

Clearly if you're a rock star and you're 27 years old, you'd better take care. If it also happens to be the 3rd of July, it could well be touch and go. In fact Brian Jones drowned in a swimming pool at his home, but his autopsy revealed that he had consumed 3.5 pints of beer or 7 whiskys along with 1,720 milligrams of an ampethamine-like substance and possibly the tranquilliser Mandrax. At least some of these may have reacted and led to his drowning. Less glamorously Jones's drowning has also been attributed to an asthma attack.

Jimi Hendrix was also a victim of drowning, but the fluid involved was his own vomit following consumption of alcohol and barbiturates. Janis Joplin died alone at the Landmark Hotel in Los Angeles of an overdose from a particularly pure batch of heroin, while Jim Morrison's death remains surrounded by mystery.

The official cause of Morrison's death is a heart attack suffered while taking a bath. The French medical authorities who dealt with the case did not find any cause to perform an autopsy. Morrison was, however, known to have been taking heroin in the days before his demise and it has been suggested that his body was placed in the bath as part of an overdose recovery procedure. Jim was also, however, a heavy drinker, and it is very possible that his death was caused by excess alcohol reacting with prescription drugs

OTHER DRUG-RELATED FATALITIES IN THE WORLD OF MUSIC

Frankie Lymon from Frankie Lymon and the Teenagers (heroin overdose), Al Wilson from Canned Heat (death attributed variously to heroin, seconal and alcohol), Danny Whitten of Neil Young's band Crazy Horse (heroin overdose, which supposedly inspired Young's song 'Needle and the Damage Done'), Tim Hardin (drug overdose suspected by some to be suicide), Tommy Bolin of Deep Purple (heroin), Paul Kossoff (drug-induced heart attack), Rick Grech of Blind Faith (overdose), Gram Parsons (body found to contain several drugs at time of death; Parsons's body was also famously stolen by his road manager, Phil Kaufman, while in transit for burial in Louisiana – knowing that Parsons had not wanted to be buried, Kaufman took the body to Joshua Tree in California and performed a cremation), Tim Buckley (snorted what he thought was cocaine at a party; it was heroin), Robbie McIntosh of the Average White Band (same reason as Tim Buckley but at a different party), Lowell George from Little Feat (heart attack induced by drug-taking), Keith Moon (reaction of anti-depressants and alcohol), Sid Vicious (heroin), John Bonham (a drug user, but it was his alcohol vomit that drowned him), Bob 'The Bear' Hite from Canned Heat (heart attack following drink and drugs), Paul Butterfield (alcohol and drugs) and Michael Bloomfield (medical condition attributed to drug abuse) both from the Butterfield Blues Band, Phil Lynott (pneumonia following years of substance abuse), Andy Gibb (heart disease following years of drink and drug abuse), Hillel Slovak of the Red Hot Chilli Peppers (heroin overdose), Stefanie Sargent of 7 Year Bitch (heroin), Johnny Thunders (heroin) and Billy Murcia (alcohol and barbiturates) both from the New York Dolls, Jerry Garcia (heart attack during period of heroin withdrawl following lifetime drug use), Andrew Wood of Mother Love Bone (heroin), Kirsten Pfaff of Hole (heroin overdose following a period of rehab), Shannon Hoon of Blind Melon (cocaine overdose), Jonathan Melvoin from Smashing Pumpkins (heroin), Dee Dee Ramone (overdose believed to be caused by heroin)... and so on.

that he was taking for asthma. The one person who might have known for definite was Morrison's wife, Pamela. She was, however, a heroin addict and herself died from an overdose in April 1975.

 ## Further rock and roll drug tragedy

Arguably drugs' more serious effect on music is the snuffing out of creative talent. Back in the 19th century Coleridge, in 'Dejection An Ode', noted that his creative powers had deserted him after little more than 10 years. In the late 1960s the stunning creativity of Brian Wilson seemed slowly to evaporate, perhaps partly as a result of his drug intake. And a comparison between works such as 'Double Fantasy' and 'The Frog Chorus' with Lennon and McCartney's earlier work might suggest that drug intake does not help creativity to flourish in the long term. Certainly the phenomenon of the acid casualty, such as Rocky Erikson of the 13th Floor Elevators, Skip Spence of Moby Grape, Arthur Lee of Love and Syd Barrett, gives drug use a bad name.

Barrett, Pink Floyd's original leader and songwriter, was by all accounts a thoroughly pleasant, outgoing and gifted young man. Syd first took LSD one day in Cambridge, some time before the Floyd established themselves as the leading lights of the London music scene in 1966–67. During his first trip Syd became incredibly interested in a plum, an orange and a matchbox and stared at these three objects for a very long time. A friend who was with him asked what he was going to do with the orange, the plum and the matchbox but was told politely to go away. In the end Syd's friend stomped on the three fascinating objects. Much later they cropped up on one of Syd's solo LP covers and in a film shown during Pink Floyd's live performances of the song addressed to Barrett, 'Shine On You Crazy Diamond'.

The other members of Pink Floyd hardly took drugs. According to drummer Nick Mason, 'Syd was a walking example of why not to.' Syd's drugs intake extended to taking acid in his coffee every morning. The drugs made him increasingly uncommunicative as the Floyd became famous around the time he was 21. Sometimes during live shows he would hardly play or sing a note but would instead stand looking blank and frightened with his Fender Telecaster hanging unused round his neck. Other times he would play one chord endlessly or detune his guitar through a song. During one show Barrett mixed Brylcreem with the drug Mandrax and spread it through his hair. Under the heat of the lights on stage, the effect appeared to some like a dribbling candle. Others were convinced that Syd's head was actually melting. After recruiting Dave Gilmour to cover for Syd, the band one day decided not to pick up their one-time leader for the gig they were on their way to. They carried on to considerable, but sadly Barrett-less, fame and fortune. While Syd's problems were probably exacerbated by his drugs intake, he almost definitely also suffered from a mental illness that would have developed in any case. Barrett nevertheless remains a fabulous talent not helped by drugs.

Giving something back

Celebrities from the world of popular music have also regularly been asked to lend their services to anti-drugs campaigns, often with bizarre results. For example, in the early 1980s, a curious line-up of musical talent was seen performing at an anti-heroin benefit at Crystal Palace in London. The appearance of Hawkwind reunited with one-time bassist and self-confessed speed-freak Lemmy might have raised a few eyebrows at such an event, but the act that followed them on stage to close the show was forces sweetheart Dame Vera Lynn singing 'We'll Meet Again'. Certainly, by the end of that show drugs simply didn't seem necessary.

During the 1960s no less a person than Elvis Presley was recruited to work as a special adviser to the Bureau of Narcotics and Dangerous Drugs. Elvis must have taken his work very seriously as he studiously went on trying every new drug launched on to the market. Elvis was reported to place orders for new types of pills after scanning through the pharmaceutical companies' latest catalogues as though they were menus.

In the USA in the late 1960s a campaign was launched to warn the youth of America against the dangers of speed. Alice Cooper recorded an anti-drugs radio message for the campaign, as did another popular artist of the day who is sadly no longer with us. 'Hi, you little assholes out there listening to the radio instead of doing your homework. This is Jim Morrison of the Doors,' began one of several aborted attempts to get an appropriate message down on tape.

Eventually Morrison came up with: 'I just got one thing to say. Don't shoot speed. Speed kills. Please don't shoot speed. Try downers, yeah, downers, barbs, tranqs, reds ... They're much less expensive.'

Overall, though, surely the most terrifying anti-drugs message ever delivered by a rock star must have been Frank Zappa's contribution to the same campaign. 'I would like to suggest that you don't use speed and here's why: it will mess up your liver, your kidneys, rot your mind,' warned Frank before delivering the final chilling thought. 'In general this drug will make you just like your father and mother.'

PUT THAT IN YOUR PIPE AND SMOKE IT

 It's amazing what you can get away with

In the absence of actual 'drug' drugs, resourceful individuals are always ready to improvise. Easily obtainable ingredients are regularly passed off as more potent substances, often with surprisingly successful results.

Gatecrashers to one Manchester college party in the early 1980s were given a warm welcome when they proffered a tin with aromatic dried weed-like substances for sharing. This 'marijuana' was prepared, smoked and enjoyed by all the revellers. Experienced dope fiends among the assembled hordes raved about the flavour and effects of this particular brand. Luckily there was a dealer operating in the

'I have in my time smoked jasmine tea, peppercorns and Bran Flakes and tried to convince myself I was getting a buzz from it.'

– David Baddiel

neighbourhood who was known to have plentiful supplies of the product. It was the Sainsbury's supermarket up the road. The noxious weed was nothing more than strands of Earl Grey tea mixed with tobacco. Chemically misguided misuse of this and other household substances seems widespread.

Ted Goldberg, on the other hand, in his book *Demystifying Drugs*, relates how a pair of cannabis dealers had established a reputation for themselves as suppliers of quality merchandise. When they suffered a shortage of the hashish they dealt, they finally decided they would have to obtain their supplies from elsewhere. So they used an iron and a wet towel to press henna hair dye into cakes. All the customers they sold the henna hash to confirmed that they had got high on it. They believed completely that their trusted dealers would not pass off inferior merchandise on them.

Nutmeg

The effect of drugs is, then, often in the eyes of the beholders, if not up their noses, in their mouths and somewhere at the back of their kitchen cupboards. Jazzman Charlie Parker may have been a wild and notorious heroin and amphetamine user, but he was also partial to the effects of an apparently innocuous cooking spice – nutmeg.

Nutmeg is the kernel of a peach-like fruit called *Myristica fragrans*. It's a familiar ingredient in the spice rack and is used by your granny to flavour custards and other dishes. Little does Granny realise, though, that she might as well be sprinkling LSD over her eggy custard. Admittedly she'd have to use quite a lot of nutmeg to achieve the same effect. Nutmeg does, however, contain psychoactive chemicals such as safrole, elemicin and myristicin. Users warn in no uncertain terms against consuming more than a tablespoonful or two at a time. It's said to cause 'intense sedation', leading to perhaps around 16 hours sleep. Vomiting and diarrhoea may, however, be as likely outcomes of a nutmeg binge as hallucinations.

Another problem with nutmeg is that it's very slow-acting. Its effects build gradually over five hours. Users are therefore tempted to up the quantity they've taken to get things moving. The result can then quite easily be a nutmeg overdose. Obviously this sounds ridiculous, but probably not if you're going through it. Besides, do you really want to be admitted to casualty suffering from a nutmeg overdose?

Back in the 15th and 16th centuries, slaves on ships carrying nutmeg would be punished for eating any of the precious cargo. Nevertheless, they were prepared to take the risk for the relief and euphoria that a few nutmeg kernels could bring.

IN the 1600s, the cocoa bean became popular not only in the form of chocolate but also as a narcotic. Cocoa contains theobromine, a chemical related to caffeine. The addictive molecules in chocolate include caffeine and another speed-like drug, phenyethylamine.

Nutmeg has also been used for its medical properties. In the last few days of his life, Charles II was given nutmeg as treatment for a haemorrhage. On the other hand, there was at one time a rumour in London that nutmegs could be used to bring on abortion. Women who sold the spice for this practice became known as 'nutmeg ladies.'

 ## Lettuce

Nutmeg is not the only staple kitchen ingredient believed by some to have a dark secret other life. Back in 1810, the Caledonian Horticultural Society went so far as to offer a prize to the person who could come up with the best method of extracting a form of 'soporific medicine' from the juice of the humble garden lettuce. These days opium lettuce is a constituent of various 'legal, herbal highs'. According to one source, all lettuces possess a form of narcotic juice, with the variety *Lactuca virosa* having the most. The heads of the plants can be cut and their juice scraped out and dried. In the ancient world, the lettuce was enjoyed for its cooling and refreshing properties, while the Roman Emperor Augustus believed it had cured him of a dangerous illness and so built an altar and erected a statue in its honour.

 ## Fish and bananas

Back in the 1960s, another readily available product was rumoured to have hallucinogenic properties. This was none other than the fruit bowl and comedy staple, the banana.

Songs from the era such as 'Mellow Yellow' by Donovan, as well as the Velvet Underground's Andy Warhol banana LP cover were rumoured to be references to the banana drug craze of the time. Country Joe, of Country Joe and the Fish fame, details the apparent beginning of the rumour:

> *Sometime around December in 1966, Country Joe and the Fish went up to Vancouver to play the Kitsilano Theatre. On the way up our drummer, Gary 'Chicken' Hirsch, said he had just figured out that banana peels have qualities similar to marijuana. His theory was that if you dried out a banana peel and smoked the white pulp on the underside, you would get high. At that time, the band was living on peanut-butter-and-banana sandwiches. All the ingredients were cheap. We were just throwing the peels away, so this sounded like a great idea.*

Country Joe and his piscine friends prepared some banana joints for themselves at a nearby psychedelic shop and were astounded by the results. They gave out banana joints at their show and told everyone they met about this hitherto overlooked property of banana skins.

A few days later, Country Joe continues,

> *[I] got up to get breakfast at the Berkeley co-op, and there were no bananas in the banana bin. I went over to Safeway and there were no bananas there either. Then I noticed a huge headline in the* San Francisco

Chronicle *that said: 'Banana Turn-on: New Hippie Craze'. Well, you couldn't get a banana in the Bay Area that day.*

The rumour spread like wildfire and persists in some quarters to this day. Unfortunately, however, bananas do not get you high. The connection Country Joe had failed to make back in the psychedelic shop in Vancouver was that while he had been preparing his banana spliffs, he had also been sipping water from a jar that a member of the Kitsilano Theatre stage crew had pointed out to him saying: 'We just dissolved a hundred tabs of LSD in that water jar. If you want any just help yourself.' This really should have given Country Joe a clue as to the actual source of the hallucinogenic effects that he attributed to the bananas. But then fish do have a notoriously short attention span.

 ## Toads

Another legendary old hippy staple is the practice of licking psychedelic poison from the skin of toads. One species of toad, the *Bufo alvarius*, is definitely known to exude a hallucinogenic chemical in its venom. If you're not prepared to sit and actually lick your toad, you can instead collect his supply of potent chemicals by milking him. This requires a glass plate, or some other non-porous surface, which is propped up in front of yourself and your toad. The toad is held in front of the plate while you work his poison glands with your fingers and thumbs. The glands on the toad's forearms, legs

TOXIC or psychoactive fungi were once believed to have been excreted by toads, hence the names 'toadstools'.

and neck should be given a gentle squeeze near their base while being aimed at your plate. So, all in all, the process is unpleasantly like squeezing a large, browny-green, toad-shaped spot into a bathroom mirror.

The resulting mixture is a milky, sticky liquid which has to be dried thoroughly before being prepared for smoking. As for your toad, you can milk him a second time after an hour's rest, but after that he should be given four to six weeks to refill his psychedelic poison pouches. The effects of toad juice have been described as pleasant and even sensual, involving possible hallucinations and a sense of well-being and oneness with nature.

Scorpions

Causing slightly more harm to the animals involved, another source of drug-like effects was recorded in Pakistan during the allied attack against the Taliban in 2001. In the temporary absence of heroin, the locals turned to scorpions. They dried the stingers from the scorpions' tails in the sun and then ground them up. The powdered venom was then smoked, the fumes being sucked down deeply into the lungs. But does it get you high? 'Oh yes,' reported one user. 'When I smoke scorpion, then the heroin is like nothing to me.'

Perhaps this explains a report on the News of the Weird website back in 1996 that US Customs had apprehended a man attempting to cross the border from Mexico carrying an ice chest containing 12,700 dead scorpions. Customs at the time were not sure if importing dead scorpions was illegal or not.

 ## Dung

A few years earlier, in Malaysia, shortages of heroin and cannabis caused addicts to resort to even more extreme methods in their attempts to get high. They took to sniffing fresh dung from the local cattle. To enjoy this delicacy the dung abusers used a coconut shell with a hole bored into the top, which was placed over cow pats. The fragrant whiffs were then snorted up through the hole. Possibly the intoxicating active ingredient in the dung was provided by the rotting vegetable material of the pat – and dung is, of course, a favoured compost for varieties of hallucinogenic fungi. Nevertheless, these Malaysians had surely taken the expression 'man, this is great shit' far too literally.

 ## Something much more extreme

In *Fear and Loathing in Las Vegas*, Hunter S. Thompson describes taking another mind-blowing, and in a sense even more readily available, substance: 'adrenochrome'. Sampling the substance which 'makes pure mescaline seem like ginger beer', he reports that there is only one source for this product: 'The adrenalin glands from a *living* human body ... It's no good if you get it out of a corpse.' Well, fresh is always best, isn't it? Thompson describes the effect being 'like a combination of mescaline and methedrine' and soon finds himself totally paralysed. 'Every muscle in my body was contracted. I couldn't even move my eyeballs, much less turn my head or talk.' The rush is so extreme that Thompson thinks the only possible outcome is death.

Maybe we shouldn't believe every word that these druggies tell us. As one authoritative internet site points out:

> *Interest in adrenochrome as a deliberately administered psychoactive is largely a persisting myth popularised by Hunter S. Thompson's writing. The oral ingestion of a vial by the main character of* Fear *and* Loathing *in* Las Vegas *is not substantiated by published research or reports, which usually refer to the endogenous metabolite.*

So it's probably not a good idea to do what Hunter S. Thompson's friend in *Fear and Loathing* suggests and chew on 'a fresh adrenalin gland'. Furthermore, while adrenochrome is a substance produced in the body, it is also the name used for a by-product of pharmaceutical epinephrine. There is a rumour that in Canada during World War Two when fresh adrenalin wasn't available hospital patients were treated with shots taken from old stock. This adrenalin had oxidised and turned slightly pink and seemed to cause temporary hallucinations. Could this tale then be the source of the persisting myth of adrenochrome consumption?

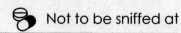 Not to be sniffed at

Unlike adrenochrome, other more mundane, readily available drug stand-ins are definitely being used – glue and gas. Cheap and readily available lighter fuel, shoe dye, petrol, nail varnish, carpet glue, contact adhesive, typewriter correction fluids, hair spray, spray paint and so on have all been used to get high. Intoxication is provided by chemicals in the substances themselves, such as butane, isobutane, propane, trichloroethylene and tetrachloroethane. Alternatively, it comes courtesy of propellant gases such as chlorofluorocarbons with which they are mixed. Unlike smoking bananas, sniffing these substances definitely does work, but, it's definitely not a good idea.

The results of solvent abuse can be a few minutes of hallucinations. As with heroin, users can pass out or go 'on the nod' and have weird dreams. Andrew Tyler's *Street Drugs* details individuals who have seen everything from babbling cartoon characters through to Roman soldiers, witches and the devil 'operating the world from an underground city where the UFOs were buried'. Coupled with the magical ability to turn stone to liquid and to pass through brick walls, this all sounds great. Unfortunately, though, it's not possible to pass through bricks walls. Nevertheless, solvent abusers have tried this and worse. Solvent sniffing is recognised by drug agencies as being as dangerous as injecting heroin.

Mystical highs

Another means of attaining drug-like altered states of consciousness is by using methods long practised by mystics and holy men of various faiths from around the world. Trances can be induced by fasting, meditation, protracted periods of isolation, repetitive chanting and/or sleep deprivation. Changes in body chemistry may also be caused by sexual abstinence, and the assumption of awkward physical postures can enable an individual to enter a trance-like state in which he loses awareness of his physical environment and attains deep spiritual revelation. Thus religious ecstasy has been attained through the ages not only by shamans and followers of Eastern faiths but also by Christian monks.

Aldous Huxley posited that the formation of adrenochrome, which is produced by the decomposition of adrenalin, might explain some mystical experiences, as its

DR John Lilly spent a lifetime investigating what happens to the brain when it is deprived of all external stimulation. To this end in 1954 he developed the world's first isolation tank. From this he discovered that sensory deprivation did not, as many scientists had supposed, put the brain to sleep. His experiments led him to conclude that the mind is not fully contained within the physical brain. The isolation tank was, he said, a 'black hole in psychophysical space, a psychological freefall', and through use of it reverie states, waking dreams and a kind of out-of-the-body travel could be achieved.

chemical composition resembles that of mescaline. Others have, however, suggested that practices such as intense prayer, meditation and chanting can produce sustained brainwaves which in turn stimulate pleasure centres in the middle region of the brain.

 ## Izzy wizzy let's get dizzy

If you want to make your head spin, you don't actually need to take any chemical substances whatsoever. You could always literally just spin your head. Making yourself dizzy is said to be one of the oldest forms of intoxication or altered states of consciousness known to man. It remains popular as an aspect of fairground rides, in ethnic dances and with small children in school playgrounds.

Young children often deliberately make themselves dizzy or even get their mates to squeeze them around the chest until they faint. According to one source, 'The panting hyperventilation, central to these effects, produces a lowering of carbon dioxide pressure, cerebral vasoconstriction, and a final dreamy collapse as the world starts to move around them.' Whirling dervishes attain altered states of consciousness by spinning, and the initiation rites of the Kung Bushmen of the Kalahari Desert also involve dancing in a

TAOIST sex techniques include the practice of partners breathing in and out of one another's throats. The build-up of carbon dioxide can begin to get them high.

circle for several hours. The dizziness produced is said to be so intense it can lead to the dancers entering a trance and seeing visions.

Making yourself dizzy may, however, like glue-sniffing, lead you to have terrible headaches, be violently sick and even accidentally smash yourself into a brick wall. Nevertheless, for ease of availability and affordability, it surely can't be beaten.

STONED TO DEATH

 OD, what can the matter be?

In case you hadn't noticed, drugs can be scary, dangerous and, at least on occasion, lethal. The ways in which they kill people can, however, be far from simple. As ever in the world of drugs, an apparently endless and varied range of reactions and unlikely occurrences may be involved.

One of the best known and most obvious ways drugs can kill you is by means of an overdose. In other words, the amount of the drug you have taken is too much for your body to bear and you find you have poisoned yourself. Drugs such as opium and cocaine were indeed once classified as poisons. A lethal dose of cocaine is estimated to be around 1 gram. There are, of course, exceptions to every rule and some individuals have been known to somehow survive 20 grams.

A lethal heroin overdose usually runs its course over a period of one to twelve hours, involving phases of shallow or irregular breathing, the skin turning blue, blood pressure dropping and coma. Most heroin overdoses are, perhaps not surprisingly, caused by injecton of the drug into the bloodstream. It has been estimated that around 2 per cent of injecting heroin users die each year.

Some drugs users die halfway through injecting themselves and are found with syringes hanging out of their arms. This seems to have been the case with Rachel Whitear, whose tragic demise was publicised by her parents in 2002 in an attempt to dissuade other young people from trying drugs. Many British newspapers published the pictures of Rachel as she was discovered in her bedsit in Exmouth, Devon, three days after her death. When she was found, she was still crouched in a kneeling position on the floor of her room with a syringe of heroin in her hand. While her stripy skirt and sleeveless cardigan looked perfectly normal, her coagulated blood had turned her flesh blue and purple. Such deaths are described as overdoses, but the fact that they occur midway through the fix rather than over a period of hours afterwards suggests they are not overdoses as such but the result of some other fatal reaction induced by the drug-taking.

The amount of each particular kind of drug required for an overdose is not set in stone. It will vary from individual to

BRITAIN'S most successful mass murderer, Dr Harold Shipman, is now thought to have killed over 200 of his patients. News reports generally refer to the fatal drug he administered to his victims as being morphine. It was in fact diamorphine, or the medically used form of heroin.

257

DATE RAPE DRUGS

It's not only the consenting user that risks being taken by surprise by drugs. Several tranquillisers have become renowned for their illicit use in knocking out a victim.

Chloral hydrate Chloral hydrate sometimes simply known as chloral was a synthetic drug widely used in the 19th century as a surgical anaesthetic and as a substance of abuse. Like so many new drugs chloral was championed following its discovery as having all the benefits and none of the problems of other narcotics. Nevertheless it destroyed, among others, the poet and painter Dante Gabriel Rossetti who became addicted to it after his wife died from an overdose of laudanum. It was also notoriously used by swindlers and rapists in the American old west.

Halcion Halcion or triazolam is a sleeping pill abused by some as a means to overcome victims. One individual known to have used the drug in this way was Jeffrey Dahmer who murdered and dismembered a series of young men during the 1980s. Typically Dahmer would pick up men from gay bars, bring them back to his flat and serve them up with a drink containing a high dose of Halcion to knock them out cold before having sex with them, strangling them, dismembering and sometimes eating them.

Rohypnol A substance marketed by Roche and created by Leo Sternbach who had previously developed Valium and Librium. Rohypnol is a benzodiazepine sedative-hypnotic that chemically resembles Valium and Librium. Rohypnol has an excellent safety record but if consumed individual and depends on such factors as body weight, metabolism, general state of health and the method by which the drug is taken. Perhaps most importantly, though, the amount required for an overdose depends on the amount an individual is used to taking or, in other words, the tolerance an individual has developed for the drug. A drug user's tolerance will also itself vary over time.

For various reasons, drug users may stop taking drugs for a period and then start up again. Unfortunately, if they start again on the same dose as they were taking when they stopped, their body's tolerance will have reduced. A dose they could once have taken safely might now be fatal. For this reason, some prisons in the United Kingdom have started a process that sounds insane to many people.

with alcohol, its effects are greatly intensified. Kurt Cobain made an unsuccessful suicide attempt using Rohypnol and champagne.

GHB GHB or gamma-hydroxybutyrate is used in some parts of the world as an anaesthetic and as an aid in child birth. In the UK it has been sold through sex shops and widely used on the London gay scene where its euphoric effects led to it becoming known as Liquid Ecstasy. Some argue that GHB's use as a date rape drug has been sensationalised by the media. Nevertheless any drug that can lead to loss of control or even to knock out the unwary can potentially be put to malicious use. In cases where GHB and Rohypnol have been used to such ends, they have usually been mixed with what may be the most widely used 'date rape drug' of them all: alcohol.

PEOPLE can and sometimes do overdose on caffeine as found in tea, coffee and soft drinks. The fatal quantity has been estimated at around 10 grams of pure caffeine, which is equivalent to 100 cups of coffee. The result of taking such an amount is likely to be fatal convulsions and respiratory failure. And that's not just from a desperate attempt to get to the toilet in time.

Before being released at the end of their sentences, prisoners with established drug habits are put through a process known as 're-toxification'. In other words, they are given drugs to build up their tolerance so they will be ready to go back out on the streets and start taking again – which will, of course, be another criminal act and could land them back in prison. No one ever claimed that the treatment of drug users made sense.

Surveys have indeed shown that the periods when heroin users are likely to overdose are during the first two weeks after release from prison and in the first year after ending treatment for addiction.

Pure

Another possible factor in drugs overdoses is the purity of the drugs that are taken. One major problem with buying drugs on the street is that there is no guarantee of what you're getting. Drug dealers do not tend to print an ingredients list or details of their customer care phone line on the side of their packs. heroin purchased in various parts of

Britain in 2002 was analysed and turned out to vary from 90 per cent down to 2 per cent pure. Ecstasy tested in the same survey was on average 25 per cent pure, and cocaine varied from 80 per cent down to 0.6 per cent pure. Heroin is referred to on the streets as 'brown' and 'white'. Evidently that's usually quite literally what you're buying – a mixture of anything as long as it's roughly the right colour.

So if the variety of heroin you are used to is 2 per cent pure and, without warning, it changes to 90 per cent pure, you're in trouble. Even if the next humble cup of coffee you glugged down suddenly turned out to be 45 times stronger than you were used to, it would probably blow your head off. The death rate among Scottish drug users rose noticeably in 1998 at the time a batch of unusually pure heroin was known to be in circulation in the area.

It was the difference in purity between New York and London heroin that is said to have killed Sex Pistols bass player and girlfriend murderer Sid Vicious. In the late 1970s, the heroin available in New York had relatively low levels of purity – perhaps around 5 per cent. It was this that Sid had got used to. A friend then brought him a special gift from England, a parcel of the much purer heroin on sale at the same time in London. The result was that, soon afterwards, Sid was Vicious no more.

'MORE Colombians die from American tobacco than the number of Americans who die from Colombian cocaine.'

– Clifford Schaffer

The mystery ingredients

The extra ingredients, or impurities, that drugs are bulked out with are potentially very dangerous in themselves. The cocaine bought on the streets of Britain in the 2002 survey turned out to have been cut with sugar, flour, talcum powder, starch and calcium silicate, a chemical normally used to treat arm injuries. Often, even the active element in 'cocaine' isn't cocaine at all but the less glamorous and much cheaper amphetamine sulphate.

The heroin samples proved to contain everything from nutmeg to brick dust, stone and ground-up glass, and the ecstasy was found to be cut with starch, talcum powder and food dye. Once ecstasy tended to circulate in the form of white tablets. Now the tablets are starting to be more colourful. This isn't just to make them look prettier though. It's so they can be cut with other materials without it being immediately apparent.

Similar studies in the past have found drug samples to be cut with rat poison, excrement, glass (again) and flour. It's probably not a good idea to stick any of this stuff into your veins. Flour may sound the least unpleasant out of the list but it has the same effect on your blood as it does when it's used to make gravy: the mixture turns unpleasantly lumpy.

Another cause of sudden upturns in the number of deaths from drugs such as heroin is sudden cuts in price. When, in 1998, heroin started appearing on the streets of Britain for the bargain price of £2, a lot of individuals with little or no previous knowledge of the drug were tempted to try it. How

PRICES FOR DRUGS IN THE UK

	1990	1997	2000	2001	Price per single hit 2001
Amphetamine (1 gram/15 lines)	£13.80	£10.00	£9.00	£9.00	£0.60
Cannabis (1 ounce/80 joints)	£91.80	£97.00	£85.00	£77.00	£0.96
Cocaine (1 gram/15 lines)	£87.00	£71.00	£65.00	£60.00	£4.00
Ecstasy (1 tab)	£18.80	£11.00	£9.00	£7.00	£7.00
Heroin (1 gram/5 doses)	£90.00	£74.00	£70.00	£63.00	£12.60
LSD (1 tab)	£4.20	£3.50	£3.30	£3.40	£3.40
Pint of lager	£1.27	£1.85	£2.02	£2.06	£2.06

(Drug prices as quoted by National Criminal Intelligence Service and in Hansard)

could they refuse at these prices? Sadly, in Norwich, for example, six people died in just one week as a result of taking cut-price heroin.

Lifestyle

It is often argued that even class A drugs are not in themselves as dangerous as the lifestyle users are forced into. It's not the drugs that kill you, it's injecting yourself with dirty needles, living in filthy circumstances, not looking after yourself properly, resorting to crime or prostitution so you can pay for your next fix, having to buy drugs from characters who don't have your best interests at heart, living alongside other extremely unhealthy drug users and so on.

Just one example of the sort of life-threatening dangers drug users can face was shown in an incidental detail in a 2002 television documentary. The Channel 4 film depicted the life of a young London heroin user called Stacey, whose existence really did seem to be a living hell. She was shown financing her heroin habit by working as a prostitute for 'city gents' while living in a dark, squalid room inside 'The Tower', a huge, derelict Victorian doss house in Whitechapel. By candlelight in her room she was filmed injecting herself with heroin, a sensation she described as like 'hot fudge ... running through my body' making her feel 'like I am lying in cotton wool ... comfortably numb to everything'. A little while later, while sitting with a friend, she sipped from a glass of water in her room only to spit it out in horror. Another friend had managed to accidentally get her blood mixed up in Stacey's drinking water. Although on this occasion Stacey survived, drug users can be killed by such casual incidents rather than by drugs themselves. On the other hand, if you

EVERY year there are at least 2,000 deaths caused by people taking aspirin and non-steroidal anti-inflammatory drugs.

ACCORDING to some experts, Elvis Presley's death on the toilet on 16 August 1977 at the age of 42 was caused by a side-effect of his addiction to prescription drugs and peanut butter and bacon sandwiches. An examination of Elvis's body found 10 different drugs in his system at the time of death, along with 14.5 kilograms (32 pounds) of impacted faecal matter in his colon. It was indeed a king-sized one. The cause of death could then have been constipation resulting from years of substance abuse which in turn triggered heart problems. Heart failure on the toilet apparently kills one in 20 people.

weren't off your head on drugs in the first place, you probably wouldn't tolerate such a lifestyle.

Another thing that kills drug users is the fact that they're not able to think straight, correctly assess risk or take the appropriate action if things start to go wrong. So, for example, one group of stoned youths watched one of their friends fall into a canal and slowly drown before their eyes. It failed to occur to any of them to do something to save him.

 ## Death by drowning

Extreme intoxication from drugs can lead to death through the rock and roll staple, drowning in one's own vomit. This was the inglorious cause of Jimi Hendrix's demise. The story goes that, after over-indulgence in alcohol and barbiturates, Hendrix fell asleep so soundly that he did not wake up even when he started throwing up. As a result, he drowned in his own vomit. Even more unpleasantly, in the film *This Is Spinal

Tap, the example is given of a musician who died as a result of drowning in vomit – but not actually his own vomit.

Another form of drowning that can be induced by drugs such as heroin is pulmonary oedema. After initial heart failure, which is after all never a good start to anything, the arteries going to the lungs become congested with blood. As the heart is unable to pump this blood away, the growing pressure eventually forces it through the capillaries and into the lungs. Thus you drown in your own bodily fluids.

Solvents solve nothing

Sniffing solvents is one of the cheaper and nastier forms of drug-taking. The ways in which solvents kill people are simultaneously unpleasant and disturbing, if not sometimes ridiculous as well. If you shoot, say, butane gas down your throat, what you are actually doing is squirting a freezing cold liquid into the vital areas inside your neck. The freezing liquid may well freeze the muscles in your throat. The result is that they will swell and choke you.

Sniffing solvents in a nice cosy confined space can also lead to another problem. After a good glue-and-gas-sniffing session, when the air is sweet with various gassy chemicals, it has been known for the assembled parties to lie back and relax. And what better way to relax than with a nice cigarette? Guess what happens when you strike a match and the room you're in is full of gas from a spray can? Sadly, some individuals get themselves to a stage where they are unable to think such things through.

STONED TO DEATH

ONE method used in the 1960s to deal with individuals suffering a bad LSD experience or 'bummer' was for everyone to gather round and demonstrate verbally and visually how much they loved the person concerned. Yup, having a bunch of hippies cluster around you while you're in the middle of a bad hallucinogenic experience didn't improve the situation in all cases.

Problems with hallucinogens

During the 1960s, taking LSD is said to have caused a group of young people to stare directly into the sun so long that they all went blind. The scientist who made this claim later admitted that he'd made the story up and that it was merely an example of what might happen. LSD has also frequently been blamed for users dying as a result of a misguided belief they could fly. The hallucinogenic drug, it is said, caused them to launch themselves off high buildings in contravention of the laws of gravity. Bill Hicks was unimpressed. 'If they thought they could fly, why didn't they take off from the ground?'

Death by ecstasy

Ecstasy can kill you for more direct reasons. Dehydration may set in as a result of ecstasy-fuelled dancing in hot and crowded locations. Sometimes a fatal heatstroke can be induced by the loss of fluid through excess sweating. This may result in convulsions, blood clotting and terminal coma.

DRUGS | A USER'S GUIDE

 ## Death by mucous membrane

Snorting is a relatively safe method of taking cocaine. This is because the membrane in the nose is quite small, so only a limited amount of the drug is allowed into your bloodstream at a time. When coke is taken through the rectum or vagina, the much larger membranes down below allow a lot more of the drug through in one go, so a dose of cocaine that may be safe when taken through the nose can turn out to be lethal if absorbed anally or vaginally. A number of women die each year for this reason. In the past some died because even their doctors didn't understand this reaction. A surgeon called Kolomnin once administered 1,530 milligrams of cocaine (the equivalent of about 30 lines) as a local anaesthetic to a female patient prior to cauterising a sore. The entire amount was absorbed into her body and the woman was dead within an hour.

 ## Show business excess

In June 1980, the comedian Richard Pryor very nearly found another way to end it all following a freebase binge at his home in Northridge, California. Having smoked all his cocaine, Pryor decided to drink the high percentage proof rum from the water pipe he'd been using. Not being totally in command of his faculties at this time, he spilt the alcohol down the nylon shirt he was wearing. At that point he decided to light a cigarette. The moment the light was struck, Pryor's rum, Pryor's shirt and Pryor's body exploded

268

into flame in rapid succession. Months of burns treatment
followed.

Even drugs that are generally thought to be relatively safe
can prove lethal in some circumstances. In 2002, in Oakland,
California, a musician called Verlon Bourn was killed as a result
of growing cannabis plants in the basement of the house
where he lived. The plants, of course, required powerful electric lights in order to grow, and Bourn had carefully set these
up all around them. But, no, it wasn't some fault with the electrical wiring that proved fatal. Verlon Bourn was shot five times
by his housemate, Andre Scott, shortly after their horrendously
expensive quarterly electricity bill dropped on the mat.

 ## A few survivors

It is possible, in ideal circumstances, to survive for years
using even the hardest hard drugs. In *Opium: A History*
Martin Booth quotes the example of an 85-year-old woman
living in the Scottish Hebrides who had been injecting heroin
for 60 years. Presumably she had outlived several dealers in
the process. Another man is known to have held down a
highly paid job as a London stockbroker despite heroin
addiction. It's fortunate for him he did have a decent job, as
his habit was costing him up to £400 a day.

'IF drugs are so bad, how come Keith Richards still walks?'

– Bill Hicks

A selection of long-lived, significant figures in the history of drugs

Thomas De Quincey, life-long opium addict (1785–1859)

Dr Timothy Leary, enthusiastic consumer and advocate of LSD and psilocybin (1920–96)

Dr John Lilly, scientific researcher who took LSD, Ketamine, etc. over protracted periods (1915–2001)

William S. Burroughs, heroin addict for many years (1914–97)

Allen Ginsberg, by his own admission stupefied on drugs from 1948 to 1963 (1926–97)

Dr Alexander Shulgin, advocate of MDMA and life-long drugs researcher (1922–)

Dr Albert Hoffmann, developer of LSD (1906–)

The charity Drugscope estimated that 2,943 deaths occurred in the UK in 1999 as a result of drug poisoning. This is undeniably a serious amount of fatalities, and each one of the individuals concerned represents a personal tragedy to their loved ones. The scale of drugs deaths, though, is vastly overshadowed by the number dying from the effects of smoking tobacco. This is estimated to be around 110,000 a year in the UK, and 400,000 a year in the USA.

GET HIP, DADDY-O

Drugs slang is as unending as the number of drug users. It seems that almost every individual who has ever rolled a joint has added to the lexicon of terms used to refer to illegal drugs. Users are apparently extraordinarily reluctant to use non-slang terms. Thus expressions such as 'Let's smoke a cannabis cigarette!' or 'Pass me the hypodermic syringe! I'm going to inject myself with heroin!' are rarely heard.

The following is, therefore, an extremely selective list of some of the more interesting drugs slang expressions, together with derivations that may not be immediately obvious and a list of some of the many different terms for the main types of drugs and the concepts associated with them.

 ## Backwashing

Rinsing out the syringe you've just used to inject drugs by drawing your blood back up into it and then injecting this back into your body. Makes sure nothing goes to waste.

Bart Simpson

A tab of acid, by virtue of the cartoon image printed on the blotting paper tab. This image is an almost endless source of slang. Any cartoon character you can think of will at one stage have been depicted on a tab of acid somewhere – the Pink Panther, Batman, Superman, Scooby Doo, etc., etc. Some users labour under the misapprehension that the picture used to decorate the tab is, somehow, related to the pretty hallucinations that the drug will induce.

 ## Billy willy

Reduction in penis size caused by taking amphetamines (amphetamines in turn being referred to as Whizz or Billy Whizz after a British comic book character).

 ## Blowback

A second person inhales someone else's exhaled smoke by placing their lips near the exhaler's.

 ## Boutros

Rhyming slang for cocaine – Boutros Boutros Gali = Charlie. Rhyming slang is another endless source of drugs slang, for example Gianlucca Vialli = Charlie, Salvador Dali = Charlie, the Republic of Mali = Charlie, and so on ad infinitum.

Burned out

Used with reference to collapsed veins no longer usable for injection.

 ## Chasing the dragon

Smoking heroin by heating the drug on foil and then inhaling the dragon-shaped fumes that rise from it.

 ## Chinese needlework

Injecting drugs.

 ## Cold turkey

Twelve hours or so after a heroin addict's last dose of the drug, the unpleasant withdrawl symptoms begin. One notable effect is the feeling of extreme cold which causes the hair on the skin to stand up and goose bumps to appear all over the body. Goose bumps are so called because of their resemblance to the skin of a dead goose but the same effect can be seen on the skin of a cold dead turkey.

 ## Crack

From the cracking sound made as this form of cocaine turns into 'rocks' – in other words, as the cocaine hydrochloride reacts with sodium bicarbonate on heating.

Crisscrossing

Setting up a line of cocaine next to a line of heroin and then snorting them with a straw into each nostril, crossing the straws halfway.

Dive

An abbreviation of 'divan', referring to the benches on which opium smokers lay in opium dens, or 'dives'.

God's Own Medicine (GOM)

Expression coined by Sir William Osler towards the end of the 19th century to describe opium. Opium was 'God's Own Medicine' because it was a natural product that seemed able to perform miracles for people suffering from an enormous range of ailments.

Hip/hippy

One often quoted derivation of these terms posits that a person who was 'hip' was originally someone who took opium. Opium was traditionally smoked while lying on one's side, on the hard wooden benches in opium dens. Once the opium took effect, the user would fall into a deep sleep for perhaps several hours. Lying repeatedly for long periods on the hard bench resulted in the user developing a sore or callus on their hip.

Another possible derivation is noted by Harry Shapiro in *Waiting For The Man: The Story of Drugs and Popular Music*. Shapiro points out that the African Wolof tribe may have been culturally dominant in early slave culture in the southern United States. The Wolof language turns out to include a number of words that could well have established themselves as slang expressions in popular music. The Wolof word *degga* means 'to understand', as in the phrase 'to dig it'. *Jev* in Wolof means 'to talk disparagingly' and may be the derivation of the word 'jive', while the Wolof expression *hipi* refers to 'a person who has opened his eyes', no doubt the way that the hippies of the 1960s would have seen themselves.

 ## Kicking the habit

About 36 hours into the process of coming off heroin, or going 'cold turkey', the body may begin to twitch and the feet kick involuntarily. At this stage you are literally 'kicking the habit'.

 ## Junky

In the early years of the 20th century, heroin addiction began to spread in the USA. There was an upsurge of heroin-related admissions at New York and Philadelphia hospitals, while throughout the east coast cities growing populations of recreational users developed.

As today, these users had to deal with the economic problems that heroin leads to. On the one hand, the user is incapable of doing very much as a result of the effects of the drug. On the other, he has to do something in order to raise money so he can afford to feed his habit.

Thus many American heroin users went into the scrap metal business. They would collect and sell scrap metal or raid yards to find material to sell. Any junk that they could sell on would suffice, and so they began to be referred to as 'junkies'.

 ## Mezz, or Mezzrow

A reefer of exceptional quality named after Milton Mezzrow, a jazz musician in the early 20th century who had been born into a Jewish family in Chicago. In the 1920s, Mezzrow became renowned in Harlem as the first marijuana dealer regularly to be able to supply quality Mexican grass.

 ## Monkey on my back

In the bebop jazz era of the 1940s and 50s musicians living with a heroin habit would say they had 'a monkey on their back'. Possibly this referred to the practice of street organ grinders carrying monkeys around with them. The monkeys would collect money from passers-by while they were, in return, looked after and fed by the organ grinder. Perhaps musicians like Charlie Parker felt that heroin addiction was the monkey that forced them out on stage to raise the cash needed to feed it.

One and one

Snorting cocaine using both nostrils.

 ## Pissed/getting pissed/ going out on the piss/pissed

This expression is used today in Britain with reference to getting drunk. According to Patrick Harding of Sheffield University, however, the phrase 'predates inebriation by alcohol by several thousand years'. What the expression in fact refers to is the ancient practice of drinking the hallucinogen-imbued urine of a tribal shaman. The shaman would have been the one person in certain ancient tribes who knew how to prepare the extremely toxic Fly Agaric mushrooms for consumption. After he had eaten the mushrooms, the other members of his tribe would enjoy the hallucinogens from the mushrooms by imbibing them after they had been filtered through the shaman. In other words, they would get high by drinking the shaman's hallucinogen-rich urine.

The effects of the drug on an individual's behaviour may also provide a link to the American expression 'pissed' (or the British equivalent 'pissed off'), a reference to someone who is annoyed or out of control.

 ## Pot

One etymologist has claimed that the word 'pot' comes from a South American drink that contained, among other things, marijuana seeds soaked in guava wine or brandy, known as *potacion de guaya*, or *potaguaya*.

Roach

The butt of a marijuana cigarette is called a roach, according to some authorities, because it looks like a cockroach. There is also a Mexican song called 'La Cucaracha' about a cockroach which is unable to walk until it has had some marijuana.

Smack

Possibly derives from the Yiddish slang word *schmecher* used to refer to an addict.

Speedball

A cocktail of heroin and cocaine, although at one time heroin and amphetamines were commonly used as the ingredients. More recently 'speedball' has been used to refer to a concoction made of ecstasy and ketamine.

Viper

Now obsolete, but a once very commonly used term for a cannabis user.

Yen

To smoke opium, from the verb meaning 'to smoke' in the Peking dialect. Nowadays to have a yen for something is to have a longing for it.

Amphetamines

Aimies, Amp, Back dex, Bam, B-bombs, Beans, Bennie, Benz, Benzedrine, Billy Whizz, Biphetamine, Black and white, Black beauties, Blackbirds, Black bombers, Black cadillacs, Black mollies, Blacks, Blue boy, Blue mollies, Bolt, Bombita, Brain pills, Brain ticklers, Brownies, Browns, Bumblebees, Candy, Cartwheels, Chicken powder, Chocolate, Christina, Coasts to coasts, Co-pilot, Crank, Crisscross, Cross tops, Crossroads, Debs, Dex, Dexedrine, Dexies, Diamonds, Diet pills, Dolls, Dominoes, Double cross, Drivers, Eye openers, Fast in, Fives, Footballs, Forwards, French blue, Gaggler, Glass, Go, Greenies, Hanyak, Head drugs, Hearts, Horse heads, Hydro, Iboga, In-betweens, Jam, Jam Cecil, Jelly baby, Jelly bean, Johnny go fast, Jolly bean, Jugs, Leapers, Lid proppers, Lightning, Little bomb, MAO, Marathons, Methedrine, Mini beans, Minibennie, Monoamine oxidase, Morning shot, Mother's little helper, Nineteen, Nugget, Oranges, Peaches, Pep pills, Pink hearts, Pixies, Pollutants, Powder, Quartz, Red phosphorus, Rhythm, Rippers, Road dope, Rosa, Roses, Snap, Sparkle plenty, Sparklers, Spivias, Splash, Splivins, Star, Strawberry shortcake, Sweeties, Sweets, Tens, The C,

Thrusters, TR-6s, Truck drivers, Turkey, Turnabout, U.S.P., Uppers, Uppies, Wake ups, West Coast turnarounds, Whiffledust, White, White Cross, Whizz, Wire

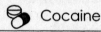

Cocaine

All-American drug, Angie, Aunt Nora, Badrock, Basuco, Batman, Bazooka, Bazulco, Beam, Berni, Bernice, Bernie, Bernie's flakes, Bernie's gold dust, Big bloke, Big C, Big flake, Big rush, Billie hoke, Birdie powder, Blanco, Blast, Blizzard, Blotter, Blow, Blunt, Bolivian marching powder, Bouncing powder, Boy, Bubble gum, Bugger sugar, Bump, Burnese, Bush, C, Cabello, Cadillac, Caine, California cornflakes, Came, Candy, Candy C, Carnie, Carrie, Carrie Nation, Caviar, C-dust, Cecil, C-game, Charlie, Chicken Scratch, Chippy, Cholly, Coca, Cocktail, Coconut, Coke, Cola, Colorado, Combol, Corrinne, Crow, Crusty treats, Crystal, Damablanca, Devil's dandruff, Double bubble, Dream, Duct, Dust, Esnortiar, Everclear, Flake, Flex, Florida snow, Foo-foo, Foo-foo dust, Foolish powder, Freeze, Friskie powder, Gift of the sun, Gift of the sun god, Gin, Girl, Girlfriend, Glad stuff, Gold dust, Goofball, Green gold, G-Rock, Gutter glitter, Happy dust, Happy powder, Happy trails, Have a dust, Heaven, Heaven dust, Henry VIII, Her, Hooter, Hunter, Ice, Icing, Inca message, Jam, Jejo, Jelly, Joy powder, Junk, King, King's habit, Lady, Lady caine, Lady snow, Late night, Late night line, Leaf, Line, Love affair, Mama coca, Marching dust, Marching powder, Mayo, Merck, Mojo, Monster, Mosquitoes, Movie star drug, Mujer,

Nieve, Nose, Nose candy, Nose powder, Nose stuff, Number 3, Oyster stew, Paradise, Paradise white, P-dogs, Pearl, Percia, Peruvian, Peruvian flake, Peruvian lady, Piece, Pimp, Polvo blanco, Powder, Powder diamonds, Press, Prime time, Quill, Racehorse Charlie, Rane, Ready rock, Rock(s), Roxanne, Rush, Schmeck, Schoolboy, Scorpion, Scotty, Serpico 21, Seven-up, She, Shot, Sleighride, Sniff, Snort, Snow, Snow bird, Snow white, Snowcones, Society high, Soda, Sporting, Star, Stardust, Star-spangled powder, Studio fuel, Sugar, Sweet stuff, T, Talco, Tardust, Teenager, Teeth, Thing, Toke, Toot, Trails, Turkey, White girl, White horse, White lady, White mosquito, White powder, Whizz bang, Wings, Witch, Yeyo, Zip

 ## Crack

151, 37461, Apple jacks, Baby T, Bad, Badrock, Ball, Base, Baseball, Bazooka, Beamers, Beans, Beat, Beautiful boulders, Bebe, Beemers, Bill Blass, Bings, Bisquits, Bjs, Black rock, Blowout, Blue, Bobo, Bolo, Bonecrusher, Bones, Boost, Botray, Boubou, Boulders, Boulya, Breakfast of champions, Brick, Bubble gum, Bullia capital, Bullion, Bump, Bumper, Butler, Caine, Cakes, Candy, Caps, Capsula, Casper the ghost, Casper, Caviar, Chalk, Cheap basing, Chemical, Chewies, Cloud nine, Cookies, Crib, Crumbs, Crunch & Munch, Cubes, Demolish, Devil drug, Devil smoke, Dice, Dime, Dime special, Dip, Dirty basing, Double yoke, Eastside player, Egg, Famous dimes, Fat bags, Fifty-one, Fish scales, Freebase, French fries, Fries, Garbage rock, Girl,

Glo, Golf ball, Gravel, Grit, Groceries, Hail, Half track, Hamburger helper, Hard ball, Hard line, Hard rock, Hell, Hotcakes, How do you like me now?, Hubba, Hubba I am back, Ice cube, Issues, Jelly beans, Johnson, Kangaroo, Kibbles 'n' Bits, Kokomo, Kryptonite, Love, Ma'a, Mixed jive, Moonrocks, New addition, Nuggets, One-fifty-one, Onion, Parlay, Paste, Patico, Pebbles, Pee-wee, Piece, Piedras, Piles, Pony, Press, Prime time, Product, Raw, Ready rock, Red caps, Regular P, Rest in peace, Roca, Rock attack, Rock star, Rocks, Rocks of hell, Rocky III, Rooster, Rox, Roxanne, Roz, Schoolcraft, Scotty, Scrabble, Scramble, Scruples, Seven-up, Sherms, Sightball, Slab, Sleet, Smoke house, Snow coke, Speed, Square time Bob, Stones, Sugar block, Swell up, Teeth, Tension, The devil, The great white hope, Tissue, Top gun, Topo, Tornado, Toss-ups, Troop, Tweaks, Twenty rock, Ultimate, Wave, Whack, White ball, White ghost, White sugar, White tornado, Wrecking crew, Yale, Yayoo, Yeah-O, Yeo, Yimyom

 ## Depressants

Backwards, Bam, Bambs, Bank bandit pills, Barb, Barbies, Beans, Black beauties, Blockbusters, Blue, Blue angels, Bluebirds, Blue bullets, Blue devil, Blue dolls, Blue heavens, Blue tips, Blue, Bombita, Busters, Candy, Chorals, Christmas rolls, Coral, Courage pills, Disco biscuits, Dolls, Double trouble, Downer, Drowsy high, GB, Gangster pills, Golf balls, Goofers, Gorilla pills, Green dragons, Green frog, Idiot pills, In-betweens, Jellies, Jelly bean, Joy juice, King Kong pills, Lay back, Lib (Librium), Little bomb, Love drug, Ludes, Luds, M&M, Marshmallow reds, Mexican reds, Mickey Finn, Mickey's, Mighty Joe Young, Mother's little helper, Nebbies, Nemmies, Nimbies, Peanut, Peter, Peth, Phennies, Phenos, Pink ladies, Q, Quad, Rainbows, Red and blue, Red bullets, Red devil, Reds, Seccy, Seggy, Sleeper, Softballs, Sopers, Stoppers, Strawberries, Stumbler, Tooles, Tooties, Tranq, Tuie, Uncle Milty, Ups and downs, Yellow bullets, Yellow jackets

 ## Heroin

Al Capone, Antifreeze, Aries, Aunt Hazel, Bad seed, Ballot, Beast, Big bag, Big H, Big Harry, Big O, Bindle, Birdie powder, Black eagle, Black pearl, Black pill, Black stuff, Black tar, Blanco, Blows, Blue bag, Blue hero, Bomb, Bombido, Bombita, Bombs away, Bonita, Boy, Bozo, Brain damage, Brea, Brick gum, Broja, Brown, Brown crystal, Brown rhine, Brown sugar, Brown tape, Bundle, Butu, Caballo, Caca, Calbo, Capital H, Caps, Carga, Carne, Chapopote, Chatarra, Cheese, Chiba, Chicle, Chieva, China, China cat, China white, Chinche, Chinese molasses, Chinese red, Chinese tobacco, Chip, Chiva, Choco-fan, Climax, Cotics, Cotton brothers, Courage pills, Crown crap, Cura, Dead on arrival, Deuce, Diesel, Diggity, Dirt, DOA, Dog food, Dogie, Dooley, Doosey, Dope, Dopium, Downtown, Dr Feelgood, Dream gum, Dream stick, Dreams, Dreck, DT, Duji, Dust, Dynamite, Dyno, Dyno-pure, Eightball, Eighth, El diablito, El diablo, Estuffa, Fachiva, Ferry dust, Fi-do-nie, Flea powder, Foil, Foo-foo stuff, Foolish powder, Furra,

Galloping horse, Gallup, Gamot, Gato, Gear, Gee, George, George smack, Girl, Glacines, Glass, God's medicine, Golden girl, Golpe, Goma, Gondola, Gong, Good and plenty, Good H, Good Horse, Goofball, Goric, Gravy, Gum, Guma, Gumball, H, H Caps, Hache, Hairy, Hammer, Hard candy, Hard stuff, Harry, Hayron, Hazel, Heaven, Heaven dust, Helen, Hell dust, Henry, Hera, Hero, Hero of the underworld, Heroina, Herone, Hessle, Him, Hocus, Hombre, Hong-yen, Hood, Hop/hops, Horning, Horse, Horsebite, Hot dope, HRN, Incense, Indonesian bud, Isda, Jee-gee, Jerry Springer, Jive, Jive doo jee, Joharito, Jojee, Jones, Joy, Joy flakes, Joy plant, Joy powder, Junco, Junk, Kabayo, Karachi, La Buena, LBJ, Lemonade, Life Saver, Little bomb, Manteca, Matsakow, Mayo, Mexican brown, Mexican horse, Mexican mud, Mojo, Moonrock, Morotgara, Mortal combat, Mud, Murder one, Muzzle, Nanoo, New Jack swing, Nice and easy, Nickel deck, Noise, Nose, Nose drops, Number 3, Number 4, Number 8, Nurse, Ogoy, Oil, Old Steve, Ope, Orange line, Outfit, Pack, Pangonadalot, Parachute, P-dope, Peg, Pen yan, Perfect High, P-funk, Pin gon, Pin yen, Poison, Polvo, Poppy, Powder, Pox, Predator, Pulborn, Pure, Quill, Racehorse Charlie, Ragweed, Rambo, Rane, Raw fusion, Raw hide, Ready rock, Red chicken, Red devil, Red eagle, Red rock, Reindeer dust, Rhine, Sack, Salt, Scag/Skag, Scat, Scate, Schoolboy, Scott, Second to none, Shit, Shmeck/schmeek, Shoot, Skee, Skid, Sleeper, Slime, Smack, Smoke, Smoking gun, Snow, Spider blue, Stuff, Sugar, Sweet dreams, Sweet Jesus, Sweet stuff, TNT, Tar, Taste, Tecate, Tecatos, Thanie, The beast, The witch, Thing, Thunder, Tigre,

Tigre Blanco, Tigre del Norte, Tongs, Tootsie roll, Toys, Train, Trash, Vidrio, Whack, When-shee, White, White boy, White girl, White horse, White junk, White lady, White nurse, White stuff, Whizz bang, Wings, Witch, Witchhazel, Yen Shee Suey, Zoquete

 ## LSD

A, Acid, Alice, Angels in a sky, Animal, Barrels, Bart Simpsons, Battery acid, Beast, Beavis & Butthead, Big D, Birdhead, Black acid, Black star, Black sunshine, Black tabs, Blackbird, Blotter, Blotter acid, Blotter cube, Blue acid, Blue barrels, Blue chairs, Blue cheers, Blue heaven, Blue microdot, Blue mist, Blue moons, Blue star, Blue vials, Brown bombers, Brown dots, California sunshine, Cap, Chief, Chinese dragons, Chocolate chips, Church, Cid, Coffee, Conductor, Contact lens, Crackers, Crystal tea, Cube, Cupcakes, D, Deeda, Dental Floss, Diablo, Dinosaurs, Domes, Doses, Dots, Double dome, El Cid, Electric Kool Aid, Ellis Day, Elvis, Felix the Cat, Fields, Flash, Flat blues, Flying triangle, Ghost, God's flesh, Golden dragon, Golf balls, Goofy's, Grape parfait, Green double domes, Green single domes, Green wedge, Grey shields, Hats, Hawaiian sunshine, Hawk, Haze, Headlights, Heavenly blue, Hits, Instant zen, L, Lason sa daga, LBJ, Leary's, Lens, Lime acid, Live, spit and die, Logor, Loony Toons, Lucy in the sky with diamonds, Mellow yellow, Mickey's, Microdot, Mighty Quinn, Mind detergent, Mother of God, Newspapers, One way, Optical illusions, Orange barrels, Orange cubes, Orange haze, Orange micro, Orange wedges, Owsley, Owsley's acid, Pane, Paper acid, Peace, Peace tablets, Pearly gates, Pellets, Phoenix, Pink blotters, Pink Panther, Pink robots, Pink wedges, Pink witches, Potato, Pure love, Purple barrels, Purple flats, Purple haze, Purple ozoline, Rainbow, Recycle, Red lips, Royal blues, Russian sickles, Sacrament, Sandoz, Smears, Snowmen, Square dancing tickets, Strawberry, Strawberry fields, Sugar, Sugar cubes, Sugar lumps, Sunshine, Superman, Tabs, Tail lights, Teddy bears, The ghost, The hawk, Ticket, Trip, Twenty-five, Uncle Sid, Valley dolls, Vodka acid, Wedding bells, Wedge, White dust, White fluff, White lightning, White Owsley's, Window glass, Window pane, Yellow, Yellow dimples, Yellow sunshine, Ying yang, Zen, Zigzag man

 ## Marijuana

420, 3750, A-bomb, Acapulco gold, Acapulco red, Ace, Afgani indica, African, African black, African bush, African woodbine, Airhead, Airplane, Alice B. Toklas, Amp, Amp joint, Angola, Ashes, Assassin of Youth, Astro turf, Atom bomb, Atshitshi, Aunt Mary, Baby, Baby bhang, Bad seed, Bale, Bamba, Bambalacha, Bammy, Banano, Bar, Bash, Bat, BC bud, Belyando spruce, Bhang, Biggy, Binky, Black, Black bart, Black ganga, Black gungi, Black gunion, Black mote, Black, Blanket, Block, Blonde, Blowing smoke, Blue de hue, Blue sage, Blunt, Bo, Bob, Bo-bo, Bobo bush, Bohd, Bomber, Bone, Boo, Boo boo bama, Boom, Broccoli, Brown, Bud, Buda, Budda, Bullyon, Burnie, Bush, Butter, Butter flower, CS, Cambodian red/Cam red, Can, Canadian black, Canamo, Canappa, Cancelled stick, Cannabis tea, Carmabis, Catnip, Cavite all star, Cereal, Cess, Cest, Charas, Charge, Cheeba, Cheeo, Chicago black, Chicago green, Chippie, Chira, Chocolate, Chocolate Thi, Christmas tree, Chronic, Chunky, Churus, Climb, Cochornis, Coli, Coliflor tostao, Colorado cocktail, Columbian, Columbus black, Corn-stalker, Cosa, Crack back, Crack weed, Crazy weed, Creeperbud, Cripple, Crying weed, Cryppie, Cryptonie, Cubes, Daddy, Dagga, Dank, Dawamesk, Dew, Diambista, Dimba, Ding, Dinkie dow, Ditch, Ditch weed, Dizz, Djamba, Don jem, Don Juan, Dona Juana, Dona Juanita, Doob, Doobie/dubbe/duby, Dope, Doradilla, Dozer, Draf, Draf weed, Drag weed, Dry high, Dube, Duby, Durog, Durong, Duros, Dust, Earth, El diablito, El diablo, Elephant, Elle momo, Endo, Esra, Fallbrook redhair, Fatty, Feeling, Fine stuff, Finger, Finger lid, Fir, Flower, Flower tops, Fraho/frajo, Frios, Fry sticks, Fu, Fuel, Fuma D'Angola, Gage/gauge, Gange, Gangster, Ganja, Gar, Gash, Gasper, Gasper stick, Gauge butt, Ghana, Giggle smoke, Giggle weed, Goblet of jam, Gold, Gold star, Golden, Gong, Gonj, Good butt, Good giggles, Goody-goody, Goof butt, Grass, Grass brownies, Grasshopper, Grata, Green buds, Green goddess, Green paint, Greeter, Greta, Griefo, Griefs, Grifa, Griff, Griffa, Griffo, Grimmy, Gunga, Gungeon, Gungun, Gunja, Gyve, Haircut, Hanhich, Happy cigarette, Harm reducer, Harsh, Has, Hash, Hawaiian Black, Hawaiian homegrown hay, Hay, Hay butt, Hemp, Herb, Herb and Al, Herba, Hit, Hocus, Homegrown, Honey blunts, Hooch, Hooter, Hot stick, Humbolt Green,

Hydro, Illies, Illing, Illy, Indian boy, Indian hay, Indian hay, Indian hemp, Indo, Indonesian bud, Instaga, Instagu, IZM, J, Jamaican gold, Jane, Jay, Jay smoke, Jim Jones, Jive, Jive stick, Joint, Jolly green, Joy smoke, Joy stick, Juan Valdez, Juanita, Juice joint, Ju-ju, Kabak, Kalakit, Kali, Kansas grass, Kate Bush, Kaya, Kee, Kentucky blue, Key, KGB, Ki, Kick stick, Kiff, Killer, Killer green bud, Killer weed, Kilter, Kind, Kind bud, King bud, Kumba, Kushempeng, Kutchie, LL, Lakbay diva, Laughing grass, Laughing weed, Leaf, Leno, Light stuff, Lima, Liprimo, Little green friends, Little smoke, Llesca, Loaf, Lobo, Loco, Locoweed, Log, Love boat, Love nuggets, Love weed, Lovelies, Lubage, M, MJ, MO, MU, Machinery, Macon, Maconha, Mafu, Magic smoke, Manhattan silver, Mari, Marimba, Mary, Mary and Johnny, Mary Ann, Mary Jane, Mary Jonas, Mary Warner, Mary Weaver, Maui wauie, Maui-wowie, Meg, Megg, Meggie, Messorole, Method, Mexican brown, Mexican green, Mexican locoweed, Mexican red, Mighty mezz, Mo, Modams, Mohasky, Mohasty, Monte, Mooca/moocah, Mooster, Moota/mutah, Mooters, Mootie, Mootos, Mor a grifa, Mota/moto, Mother, Mr Lovely, Mu, Muggie, Muggles, Muta, Mutha, Nail, Nigra, Number, OJ, Oboy, One hitter quiter, Oolies, Owl, Ozone, PR, Pack, Pack a bowl, Pack of rocks, Pack, Pakalolo, Pakistani black, Panama cut, Panama gold, Panama red, Paper blunts, Parsley, Pasto, Pat, Pin, Pine, Pizza, Plow, Pocket rocket, Pod, Poke, Pot, Potlikker, Potten bush, Prescription, Pretendica, Pretendo, Primo, Queen Ann's lace, Railroad weed, Rainy day woman, Rangood, Rasta weed, Red bud, Red cross, Red dirt, Reefer,

Regs, Righteous bush, Rip, Roacha, Rockets, Rompums, Root, Rope, Rose marie, Rough stuff, Rubia, Salt and pepper, Santa Marta, Sasfras, Scissors, Seeds, Sen, Sess, Sezz, Shake, Shmagma, Shrimp, Siddi, Sinse, Skunk, Smoke, Smoke a bowl, Smoke Canada, Smoochywoochy-poochy, Snop, Speedboat, Splaff, Spliff, Splim, Square mackerel, Stack, Stems, Stick, Stink weed, Stoney weed, Straw, Sugar weed, Super pot, Supergrass, Sweet Lucy, T, Taima, Takkouri, Tea, Texas pot, Texas tea, Tex-mex, The Dank, Thirteen, Thumb, Tia, Torch, Torpedo, Trees, Trupence bag, Turbo, Tustin, Tweeds, Twist, Twistum, Twisty, Unotque, Viper, Viper's weed, Wacky weed, Wake and Bake, Water-water, Weed, Weed tea, Whackatabacky/Whacky backy, Wheat, White-haired lady, Woollies, Woolly blunts, Wooz, Wuwoo, X, Yeh, Yellow submarine, Yen pop, Yeola, Yerba, Yerhia, Yesca, Yesco, Ying, Zacatecas purple, Zambi, Zigzag man, Zol, Zoom

MDMA

A bean, Adam, Baby slits, Batmans, Bibs, Biphetamine, Blue kisses, Blue lips, Booty juice, Chocolate chips, Clarity, Cloud nine, Cristal, Dead road, Debs, Deccadence, Dex, Dexedrine, Diamonds, Disco biscuits, Doctor, Dolls, Drivers, E, E-bombs, Ecstasy, Egyptians, Elaine, Essence, Eve, Exiticity, Fastin, Flower flipping, Gaggler, Go, Greenies, Gum, GWM, H-bomb, Hammerheading, Happy drug, Happy pill, Herbal bliss, Hug drug, Hydro, Iboga, Kleenex, Letter biscuits, Love doctor, Love drug, Love potion #9, Lover's speed, Lucky

Charmz, MAO, MDM, Methedrine, Mini beans, Molly, Monoamine oxidase, Morning shot, Nineteen, Number 9, Pollutants, Rave energy, Rib, Ritual spirit, Roca, Roll, Rolling, Running, Scooby snacks, Slammin'/Slamming, Slits, Speed for lovers, Spivias, Strawberry shortcake, Sweeties, Tens, Tutus, Tweety birds, USP, Ultimate Xphoria, Vitamin E, Wafers, West Coast turnarounds, Wheels, Whiffledust, White dove, Wigits, X, X-ing, X-pills, XTC

 ## To inject drugs

Bang, Bingo, Blow the vein, Boost, Boot, Burn the main line, Cooker, Crank up, Dig, Draw up, Dropper, Dry up, Fire, Fix, Geeze, Geeze a bit of dee gee, Get down, Get off, Go into a sewer, Gravy, Gun, Hit the main line, Hit the needle, Hit the pit, Hit up, Jab/job, Jack up, Jolt, Joy pop, Laugh and scratch, Mainline, Miss, Ping-in-wing, Pin, Poke, Shoot/shoot up, Skin pop, Slam, Spike, Tie, Track

 ## To smoke marijuana

Bite one's lips, Blast, Blast a joint, Blast a roach, Blast a stick, Blaze, Blow a stick, Blow one's roof, Boot the gong, Burn one, Do a joint, Dope smoke, Fire it up, Fly Mexican airlines, Get a gage up, Get high, Get the wind, Go loco, Hit, Hit the hay, Mow the grass, Poke, Puff, Puff the dragon, Spark it up, Tea party, Toke, Toke up, Torch up

GET HIP, DADDY-O

 ## A marijuana cigarette

Ace, African woodbine, Binky, Blanket, Bob, Bomber, Camberwell carrot, Cancelled stick, Catnip, Climb, Cripple, Daddy, Earth, Fatty, Finger, Gasper, Gasper stick, Golden leaf, Good butt, Goof butt, Gyve, Happy cigarette, Hawaiian, Hay butt, Hit, Hot stick, J, Jay, Joint, Joy stick, Ju-ju, Kaff, Khayf, Kick stick, Kiff, Log, Mari, Megg, Mighty mezz, Mooters, Nail, Number, Pack of rocks, Prescription, Reefers, Rockets, Spliff, Straw, Twist, Twistum, Twisty, Zol

 ## Under the influence of drugs

All lit up, Amped, Amped and queer, Baked, Banging, Belted, Blasted, Blitzed, Blown, Booted, Buzzing, Chalked up, Charged up, Coasting, Dusted, Faded, Flying, Gacked, High, Hopped up, Keyed, Leaping, Lifted, Lit, Lit up, Loaded, On a trip, On one, On the nod, Permafried, Razed, Red, Riding the wave, Ripped, Shot down, Skied, Smoked-out, Spaced out, Stoned, Trashed, Tripping, Wasted, Weightless, Wired

 ## To inhale cocaine

Blow blue, Blow coke, Blow smoke, Booster, Cork the air, Do a line, Geeze, Go on a sleigh ride, Hitch up the reindeers, Horn, One and one, Pop, Sniff, Snort, Toke, Toot

A hypodermic syringe

Glass, Fuete, Gaffus, Glass, Glass gun, Hype stick, Sharps

Equipment used to take drugs

Artillery, Kit, Lay-out, Rig, Tools, Works

An addict

Ad, Binger, Chaser, Gutter junkie, Hype, Junkie, Klingon, Nickelonian, Rock fiend, Smack head

Addicted to drugs

Hooked, Up against the stem

Cocktail hour

Of course, mixing drugs with each other or even with just good old-fashioned and perfectly legal alcohol is usually an excellent way to make their effects considerably more unpredictable and even potentially lethal. Finally, here are a few names of druggy combinations and their ingredients:

Atom bomb: marijuana and heroin
B-40: cannabis cigar dipped in malt liquor
Backbreakers: LSD and strychnine
Belushi: A speedball of heroin and cocaine named in honour

of actor John Belushi, who was supposedly killed by such a cocktail

Bhang Lassi: Indian yogurt and cannabis drink

Blunt: marijuana and cocaine

Boat: PCP and marijuana

Chocolate ecstasy or chocolate rocket: crack with chocolate milk powder

Chronic: cannabis and crack

CK1: cocaine and ketamine (named after the perfume)

Clicker: crack and PCP

Coco rocks: crack turned dark brown by a dash of chocolate pudding

Cocoa puff: cocaine and marijuana

Coolie: tobacco and cocaine cigarette

Corn-stalker: cannabis joint rolled in the leaves of a corn cob and sealed with honey

Cotton brothers: cocaine, heroin and morphine

Crack back: crack and marijuana

Croak: crack and methamphetamine

Crystal pop: cocaine and PCP

Cut-deck: heroin with powdered milk

Dip: cigarettes dipped in embalming fluid

Double rock: crack diluted with procaine

El diablito: marijuana, cocaine, heroin and PCP

El diablo: marijuana, cocaine and heroin

Elle Momo: marijuana laced with PCP

Euphoria: MDMA, mescaline and crystal meths

Fire: crack and methamphetamine

Flat chunks: crack and benzocaine

Frios: marijuana with PCP

Frisco special or Frisco speedball: cocaine, heroin and LSD

Fry: crack or marijuana with embalming fluid or acid

Fry daddy: crack and marijuana; cigarette laced with crack

Geek: crack and marijuana

Gimmie: crack and marijuana

Goofball: cocaine and heroin

Herb and Al: cannabis and alcohol

Honey blunts: cannabis cigars sealed with honey

Lace: cocaine and marijuana

New Jack Swing: heroin and morphine

Outerlimits: crack and LSD

Parachute: crack and PCP

P-funk: crack and PCP

Reekstick: tobacco laced with cocaine

Sheet rocking: crack and LSD

Shermans: cigarette with PCP

Smoke: heroin and crack

Snow seals: cocaine and amphetamine

Snowball: cocaine and heroin

Space base or space cadet: crack dipped in PCP

Speedball: heroin and cocaine, although at one time heroin
and amphetamines were commonly used as the ingredients. More recently, though, a 'speedball' has referred to
a combination of ecstasy and ketamine.

Splaff: cannabis joint with a hint of LSD

Torpedo: crack and marijuana

Tragic magic: crack dipped in PCP

Turbo: crack and marijuana

Wac: PCP on marijuana

Whack: PCP and heroin

Whiz bang: cocaine and heroin

Wild cat: methcathinone and cocaine

Woollies: marijuana with a soupçon of crack or PCP

Woolly: cocaine and marijuana joint

Woolly blunts: marijuana with crack or PCP

Wuwoo: marijuana and cocaine

HUBBLY-BUBBLY-OGRAPHY

Stephen Arnott, *Now Wash Your Hands*, 2001

Virginia Berridge, *Opium and the People*, 1999

Martin Booth, *Opium: A History*, 1996

Andrew Calcutt and Richard Shephard, *Cult Fiction: A Reader's Guide*, 1998

John Cohen (editor), *The Essential Lenny Bruce*, 1973

Rupert Davenport Hines, *The Pursuit of Oblivion: A Global History of Narcotics*, 2001

Julian Durlacher, *Agenda: Heroin*, 2000

Julian Durlacher, *Agenda: Cocaine*, 2000

Ted Goldberg, *Demystifying Drugs: A Psychosocial Perspective*, 1999

Jim Hogshire, *Pills A Go Go*, 2001

International Times, *The IT Book of Drugs*, 1971

Miriam Joseph, *Agenda: Ecstasy*, 2000

Miriam Joseph, *Agenda: Speed*, 2000

Robert Lacey and Danny Danziger, *The Year 1000*, 1999

Grevel Lindop, *The Opium Eater*, 1985

Howard Marks (editor), *The Howard Marks Book of Dope Stories*, 2001

Patrick Matthews, *Cannabis Culture*, 2000

Nicholas Saunders, Anja Saunders and Michelle Pauli, *In Search of the Ultimate High*, 2000

Harry Shapiro, *Waiting for the Man*, 1986

John Simpson, *A Mad World, My Masters*, 2001

Dominic Streatfield, *Cocaine: An Unauthorised Biography*, 2000

Andrew Tyler, *Street Drugs*, 1986

Stuart Walton, *Out of It*, 2001

Geoffrey C. Ward/Ken Burns, *Jazz*, 2001

INDEX

INDEX

INDEX

INDEX

INDEX